Brickwork 1

by the same author

Brickwork 2
Brickwork 3
Brickwork Bonding Problems and Solutions

Brickwork 1

Third Edition

W. G. Nash, MCIOB

Stanley Thornes (Publishers) Ltd

Originally published in 1966 by Hutchinson Education
Second edition 1969
Reprinted 1974, 1975 (twice), 1977, 1979, 1980, 1981, 1982
Third edition 1983
Reprinted 1985, 1986 (twice), 1987, 1988, 1989

Reprinted again in 1989 by
Stanley Thornes (Publishers) Ltd
Old Station Drive
Leckhampton
CHELTENHAM GL53 0DN

British Library Cataloguing in Publication Data

Nash, W. G.
   Brickwork.—3rd ed.
   1
   1. Bricklaying
   I. Title
   693′.21   TH5501

   ISBN 0 7487 0266 0

Set in Linotron Times

Printed and bound in Great Britain at
The Bath Press, Avon

Contents

Preface

In order to maintain the general rise in our standard of living, new ideas and techniques must be introduced into the construction industry. These can only be implemented if there are skills enough to carry out the requirements of the technologist, so that the craftsman is still all-important, and is likely to remain so.

It may be argued that methods which have been used for many years cannot be improved upon, and, indeed, it has been found extremely difficult to reduce the cost of a house built with the traditional brick walls. But new ideas and methods which will change this situation may well be forthcoming. The well-trained craftsman will always be on the alert to observe and study techniques which help to increase productivity. The less-able craftsman, however, may not be able to change in quite the same way because he lacks the basic training. The fundamental principles of any craft must be thoroughly understood before it is possible to start any schemes for improving methods. There is no doubt that the building industry will see some tremendous changes in the future. The good craftsman will always be ready to meet this challenge.

This volume has been set out to give an understanding of the basic principles of the craft of bricklaying; it has been devised to cover the preliminary requirements of those embarking on a career in the construction industry.

The self-assessment questions at the end of each chapter will be suitable for those attending the first and second years of the City and Guilds brickwork course. They are designed to test the reader's knowledge of the subject in each chapter and also to create interest so that students may continue their investigations and extend the work already covered.

I would like to acknowledge the advice and help which I have received from Mr V. Pannell, lecturer in brickwork and associated subjects at Southampton Technical College, in the revision of this volume.

Finally, I hope that this book will be of great use to students or apprentices about to start on their careers in the construction industry. May they find pleasure, interest and much satisfaction in all their work.

W. G. Nash
1983

Metrication tables

Table 1 *Basic units*

Quantity	Unit	Symbol
length	metre	m
mass	kilogramme	kg
time	second	s
electrical current	ampere	A
temperature	degree Celsius, kelvin	°C, K
luminous intensity	candela	cd

Table 2 *Derived* SI *units with special names*

Quantity	Unit	Symbol
force	newton	N
work, energy	joule	J
power	watt	W
electrical potential	volt	V
luminous flux	lumen	lm
illumination	lux	lx

Table 3 *Derived* SI *units with complex names*

Quantity	Unit	Symbol
area	square metre	m^2
volume	cubic metre	m^3
frequency	cycle per second, hertz	Hz
density	kilogramme per cubic metre	kg/m^3
velocity	metre per second	m/s
pressure, stress	newton per square metre	N/m^2
thermal conduc-tivity	watt per metre kelvin	W/mK
luminance	candela per square metre	cd/m^2

Table 4 *Multiples and sub-multiples of* SI *units*

Multiplication factor		Prefix	Symbol
1000 000	10^6	mega	M
1000	10^3	kilo	k
100	10^2	hecto	h
10	10^1	deca	da
0.1	10^{-1}	deci	d
0.01	10^{-2}	centi	c
0.001	10^{-3}	milli	m
0.000 001	10^{-6}	micro	μ

Chapter 1

Bricks and their manufacture

After reading this chapter you should be able to:

1 Have an understanding of the processes involved in the manufacture of bricks.

2 Understand the difference between machine-pressed and wire-cut bricks.

3 Have an understanding of various types of kilns.

4 Compare the production of clay bricks with sand-lime bricks.

5 Have a knowledge of the production of concrete bricks.

You, the craftsman, need sound knowledge of your materials; you are responsible for the handling and fixing of them. You must know not only your own materials but also those you may meet when working with other crafts. Ignorance can spoil materials and increase the final cost of a job in time and replacements.

Since the building industry constantly changes and introduces new ideas in construction, the good craftsman makes it part of his business to keep up to date with information about the new and existing materials and methods of fixing.

Research work is often conducted by industry and government research stations, and the results are published and passed on to building firms. Technical colleges are constantly receiving information from these centres; they can pass the new ideas to students, so that in the building crafts the apprentices have a good opportunity of keeping up to date with information, especially with the scientific developments in materials.

Bricks

Bricks may be classified as being among the most durable of building materials. Indeed, throughout the country we have many excellent examples of brickwork which have survived for hundreds of years. Some buildings have bricks made by the Romans which are still in a first-class condition today. The Romans were excellent builders and engineers, and the structures which can be seen in many parts of the British Isles are testimonies to their skill.

Bricks were in use long before the Roman era; in fact, their use is recorded in the ancient city of Babylon about 6000 years ago, and the Bible mentions several times the making of bricks. You probably know the story of the Israelites, who, as slaves, were expected by their Egyptian conquerors to 'make bricks without straw'.

An interesting thing about bricks is that their size has not varied greatly through the ages. The greatest variation appears to be in the depths of the bricks and this seems to be mainly controlled by their weight. Each brick should be light enough to be handled with one hand without causing excessive fatigue before the day's work is finished. The width is determined by the need for convenient handling and has remained fairly constant at about 100–125 mm. Although the width and length of bricks remain fairly uniform throughout the country, the depth can vary from 50 to 80 mm.

The majority of bricks in this country are made from clay, and because of the different types of clay which exist, a wide variety of different bricks is available, with a remarkable selection of colours, including near white, grey, blue to near black, brown, orange and red. The weight of the bricks ranges from about 1 kg to nearly 5 kg. Some absorb much water, others absorb little or no water at all. Some are square with regular *arrises*, others are irregular. Most are now machine-made but a few are still made by hand. A line diagram showing the manufacture of clay bricks is shown in Figure 1.

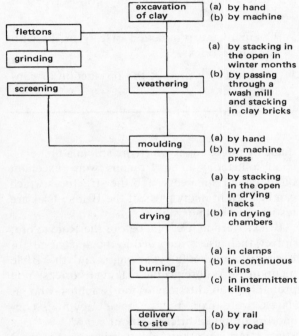

Figure 1 *Clay bricks*

Processes of manufacture

Preparing the clay
Before some types of clay bricks are made, the clay is *weathered*. In one method it is stacked in heaps in the open for the rain to wash out the soluble salts, which might later cause efflorescence or white scum on the face of the brickwork. Another method is to wash the clay thoroughly in a wash-mill and then store it in large open storage areas called clay *backs* until ready for use.

Other types of clay bricks, such as flettons, are made from unweathered clay. The clay is dug and immediately transported to the grinding mill where a very small amount of water is added and the clay is ground finely, before passing on to the brick-making machines.

Machine-pressed bricks
Some brick-making machines require the clay to be *pugged* with water before moulding. Others, such as those for making fletton bricks, require a semi-dry clay. But the principle in all cases is similar: the clay is fed into moulds and then pressed into the shape required. The greater the pressure, the denser will be the resultant brick. Fletton bricks are pressed four times because of the nature of the clay, but usually a single press is sufficient for bricks made with pugged clay (Figure 2(a)).

Wire-cut bricks
Another type of machine is required to make wire-cut bricks. The clay is pugged and forced through an opening, which is approximately 240 by 125 mm (the extra size is to allow for shrinkage in the clay during burning), and emerges as a long continuous slab to be cut into 75 mm thick slabs by means of wires attached to a frame. After completion these are usually sold as *wire-cuts*. Sometimes the wire-cut bricks are fed into a press, and *frogs* forced in under pressure, which gives the bricks greater density; the resulting bricks are sold as pressed *facings* (see Figure 2(c)).

Drying
The freshly made or *green* bricks must be thoroughly dried before burning, and this can be done in two different ways:

1 Storing them in the open air in long rows called *drying hacks*, where the bricks are stacked on edge about seven courses high, with temporary wooden covers over them as protection against wind and rain, to keep the drying as constant as possible.
2 Stacking them in drying chambers.

The first method is slower and is completely dependent upon the weather conditions. The drying time is from six to ten weeks. The second method is more controlled, and takes just a few

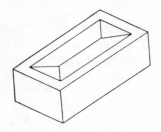

(a) pressed brick — clean, sharp edges, regular in shape and uniform in size

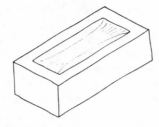

(b) hand-made brick — edges not sharp, irregular shape and not uniform in size. Frogs irregular in shape

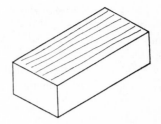

(c) wire-cut bricks — sharp edges, no frogs and wire can often be seen on a bed of bricks

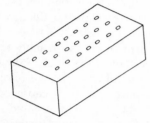

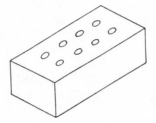

(d) types of perforated bricks

Figure 2

days. The drying operation is important because if the bricks were burnt in a damp condition they would twist, warp and crack and be generally useless for ordinary walling.

Burning

After the 'green' bricks are thoroughly dried they are burnt at a high temperature. The following are the more common types of kiln used for this operation:

Clamp
Scotch
Down-draught
Hoffman
Continuous

Kilns

Clamp

This is an intermittent method of burning, that is, the kiln is loaded with green bricks and then they are burnt. The fires are then allowed to burn out and the bricks unloaded. The cycle of operations is repeated.

The kiln consists of a rectangular base with

fireholes, which are filled with coke breeze. The clay for making the bricks also has coke breeze mixed with it during the weathering process. The dried, unburnt or green bricks are stacked on edge in walls or bolts of about 3 metres high on top of the coke breeze which is spread at the base of the kiln. The outer faces of the clamp are stacked so that they lean inwards. Underburnt bricks are finally stacked on the sides and top of the kiln to protect the bricks in the kiln from being affected by rain and wind.

The breeze at the base of the clamp is ignited, and as the temperature gradually rises, the breeze, which was mixed with the clay in the bricks, also ignites; thus the chemical compounds in the clay are changed by the heat, resulting in a hard, dense product.

Clamp-burnt bricks can sometimes be recognized by the small patches of burnt breeze visible on their surfaces.

Scotch kiln

The method of burning bricks in this type of kiln is somewhat similar to clamp-burning, except that the bricks are burnt within four walls, with an opening at one end which is sealed up during the burning; coal is fed through fireholes at the bottom of the two side walls. A layer of underburnt bricks from a previous burning is placed right over the top of the green bricks to protect them from the weather during burning (Figure 3(a)).

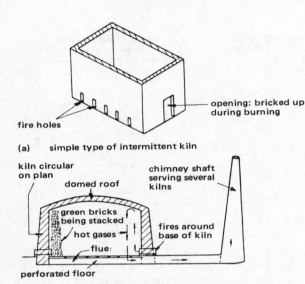

fire holes

opening: bricked up during burning

(a)   simple type of intermittent kiln

kiln circular on plan

domed roof

chimney shaft serving several kilns

green bricks being stacked

hot gases

fires around base of kiln

flue

perforated floor

(b)   down-draught intermittent kiln

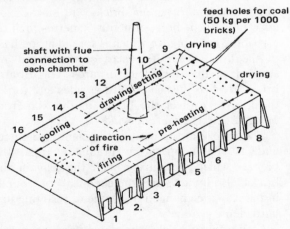

feed holes for coal (50 kg per 1000 bricks)

shaft with flue connection to each chamber

drying

drying

direction of fire

drawing setting

pre-heating

cooling

firing

(c)   Hoffman continuous kiln

Typical order of operating:

1, 2, 3 firing. Coal fed from top
4, 5, 6, 7 pre-heating bricks
8, 9, 10 drying green bricks
11 setting kiln with green bricks
12 drawing burnt bricks and loading on lorries
13, 14, 15, 16 cooling burnt bricks

Figure 3   *Types of kilns*

Down-draught kiln

This is circular with a domed roof, fireholes spaced around the base of the wall, and one opening, which is sealed during the burning process, for access. The floor of the kiln is perforated and connected by flues to a chimney shaft. Coal is generally the fuel which is used for burning, but in recent years oil has been introduced. When the kiln is loaded the opening is sealed and the fires lit. On firing at high temperatures, the colder gases being more dense force the hotter gases up to the roof, and as the cooler gases travel downwards, so they pass through the perforated floor into the shaft and out through the flue. A high temperature can be reached with this type of kiln, producing a hard-burnt brick and usually taking up to about ten days to burn the bricks from start to finish. This type of kiln is used also for the manufacture of salt-glazed ware because of the high temperatures that can be achieved and is not entirely suitable for high brick output (Figure 3(b)).

Hoffman kiln

This is a continuous kiln, that is, the fire never goes out as it is transferred from one chamber to another. To facilitate loading and unloading, the kiln is divided into a number of separate chambers, usually sixteen, having eight on each side with dampers between them which may be opened for the fire to pass from one chamber to the next. All the chambers in one kiln are connected to a single chimney shaft. As the fire passes round the kiln so the chambers in front of the actual firing zone are gradually warmed, and the chambers behind cool off slowly. Although the burning time is only about three days, the bricks are in the kiln for about ten days to allow for raising the temperature and, after burning, subsequent lowering of the temperature before unloading the chambers. This type of kiln is used for the burning of fletton bricks (Figure 3(c)).

Continuous kiln

In this type of kiln the green bricks are loaded on to steel trucks which form a continuous line, and pass into a long chamber which has a firing zone in the middle of its length. The trucks are slowly passed through the kiln, gradually warming as they reach the firing zone; then they are burnt, and gradually cool off somewhat before emerging at the far end of the kiln.

Types of bricks

Clay bricks

These are broadly divided into three groups as follows:

1 *Common bricks*, which have no particular finish on any surface, and are generally intended for use on internal work or any work which is to be covered, or where the appearance is of secondary importance.
2 *Facing bricks*, which have a finished surface, either sanded or smooth textured. They may be uniform in colour or multicoloured; they also vary considerably in density. They are used for facing buildings, and to provide a durable and pleasing finish.
3 *Engineering bricks*, which are very dense and are used for:

walls or piers which have to carry heavy loads
retaining walls
bridge abutments and piers
lining of concrete chimney shafts

brick sewers and any type of walling which may be subject to exposure, abrasion or acid attack

British Standard Specification BS 130 covers the minimum requirements of engineering bricks, and includes their classification, compressive strength and water absorption.

Firebricks

These are special bricks for lining chimney shafts, boilers and kilns, or for any work where resistance to heat is required. The clay used for the making of these bricks is called a refractory clay, which means that it will resist heat or withstand a high temperature. The firebricks are bedded in a thin layer of refractory mortar which is mixed to a slurry and placed in a shallow box. The bricks are dipped into the slurry and then laid, with very thin joints between them.

Sand-lime bricks (calcium-silicate bricks)

These are made in a different way from clay bricks. The materials used are lime and sand in the proportion of about 1:8, mixed together with a very small amount of water. This damp mixture is moulded under great pressure into the required brick shapes. The green bricks are loaded on to

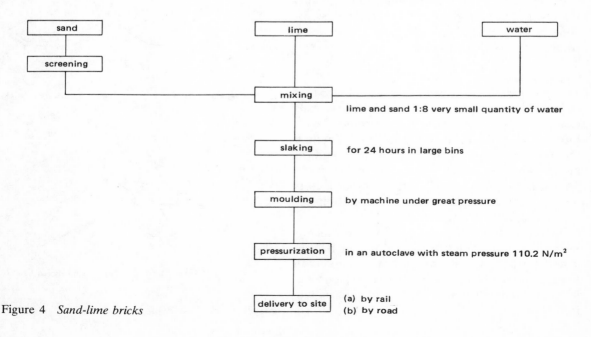

Figure 4 *Sand-lime bricks*

trucks and these in turn are pushed into *auto-claves* which are huge steel 'pressure cookers'. When the autoclave is loaded, the steel cap is bolted on to the end and steam is injected into the chamber until a pressure of about 110.24 N/m² is reached, and is maintained for seven or eight hours. This means that each brick has a total force of approximately 1.016 tonnef over all its surface area. This pressure combined with the heat and steam causes the sand and lime to combine chemically, so when the bricks are unloaded and allowed to cool down they are ready for use. An outline of the process is shown in Figure 4.

There are four classes of sand-lime bricks:

1   Bricks for special purposes suitable for use in work where a high strength is required, or subject to continuously becoming saturated with water, or liable to be exposed repeatedly to temperatures below freezing when saturated with water.
2   Building bricks suitable for general external facing work.
3   Building bricks suitable for general external facing work in mortars other than strong cement mortar.
4   Building bricks suitable only for internal work in mortars other than strong cement mortars.

BS 187 deals with the minimum requirements for these bricks and covers their dimensions, appearance, crushing strength, transverse strength and drying shrinkage.

Concrete bricks

The method of manufacture is similar to that described for sand-lime bricks, but the materials used are cement and sand (or air-cooled blast-furnace slag). BS 1180 deals with the minimum requirements for these bricks and the classification of the types, which is the same as that listed for sand-lime bricks, and mentions other factors such as materials, dimensions, curing, compressive strength and drying shrinkage.

Another type of concrete brick is one which is made with cement and furnace clinker or fly ash. These bricks are built into various positions in walling so that picture rails, skirtings, serving-hatches and door frames can be secured by nailing into them.

The brick-making industry is very large and involves the use of much capital equipment, and as it is only possible to give an outline on this subject, you are recommended to visit works to see local methods of brick manufacture.

Purpose-made bricks

In addition to the various shapes obtained by cutting, there are many bricks which are made for special purposes and may be purchased from the makers. Figures 5–9 show some examples of these.

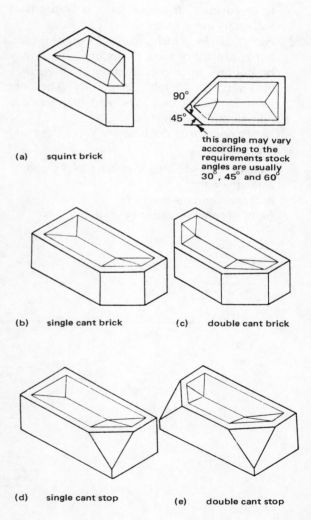

Figure 5   *Purpose-made bricks*

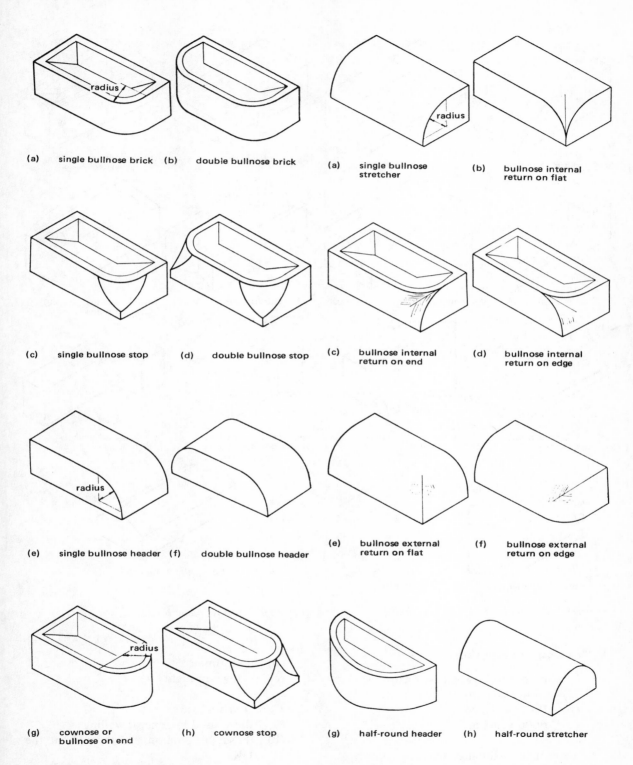

(a)   single bullnose brick   (b)   double bullnose brick

(a)   single bullnose
       stretcher

(b)   bullnose internal
       return on flat

(c)   single bullnose stop   (d)   double bullnose stop

(c)   bullnose internal
       return on end

(d)   bullnose internal
       return on edge

(e)   single bullnose header (f)   double bullnose header

(e)   bullnose external
       return on flat

(f)   bullnose external
       return on edge

(g)   cownose or
       bullnose on end   (h)   cownose stop

(g)   half-round header

(h)   half-round stretcher

Figure 6   *Purpose-made bricks*

Figure 7   *Purpose-made bricks*

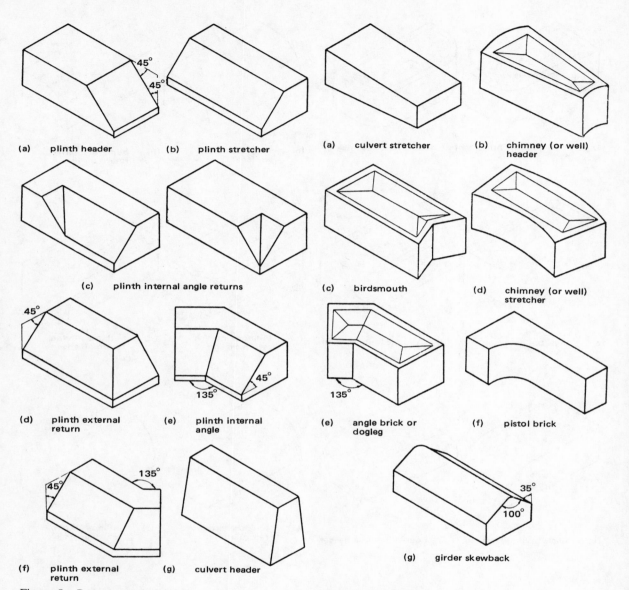

(a)   plinth header   (b)   plinth stretcher

(c)   plinth internal angle returns

(d)   plinth external   (e)   plinth internal
       return   angle

(f)   plinth external   (g)   culvert header
       return

Figure 8   *Purpose-made bricks*

(a)   culvert stretcher   (b)   chimney (or well)
                                       header

(c)   birdsmouth   (d)   chimney (or well)
                                       stretcher

(e)   angle brick or   (f)   pistol brick
       dogleg

(g)   girder skewback

Figure 9   *Purpose-made bricks*

Self-assessment questions

1   The use of bricks was first recorded
     (a)   500 years ago
     (b)   1000 years ago
     (c)   6000 years ago

2   Fletton bricks are fired in
     (a)   an intermittent kiln
     (b)   a Hoffman kiln
     (c)   a down-draught kiln

3   Common bricks are
     (a)   those used in general walling
     (b)   those in common use throughout the
            UK
     (c)   those having the same dimensions

4   Sand-lime bricks are heated in
    (a)   intermittent kilns
    (b)   autoclaves
    (c)   clamps

5   Sand-lime bricks for special purposes are
    (a)   those having special shapes
    (b)   those for use where work of high strength is required
    (c)   those for use in general external facing work

6   Bricks should be thoroughly dried before burning to
    (a)   ensure even colour
    (b)   ensure easy handling
    (c)   prevent cracking

7   The shaped brick shown in Figure 10 is
    (a)   a squint brick
    (b)   a cant brick
    (c)   a bullnose brick

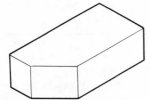

Figure 10

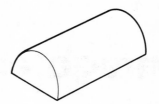

Figure 11

8   The brick shown in Figure 11 is
    (a)   a half-round header
    (b)   a bullnose brick
    (c)   a half-round stretcher

9   Sand-faced flettons are produced by
    (a)   sprinkling the burnt bricks with sand and re-burning
    (b)   sand blasting the green bricks before burning
    (c)   using a sandy clay to make the bricks

10 Why is clay intended for brickmaking, weathered?

11 Why should bricks be burnt at a high temperature?

12 Make neat sketches of the following special bricks
    (a)   an internal plinth
    (b)   an external plinth

Chapter 2

Aggregates

After reading this chapter you should be able to:

1 Understand the difference between coarse and fine aggregates.
2 Appreciate the ratio of surface area to volume in various sizes of aggregates.
3 Understand why it is so important to have a correct balance of surface area of aggregate with cement to achieve the required strengths in mortars and concrete.
4 Comprehend why impurities should not be present in aggregates which are intended for concrete.
5 Have a knowledge of various categories of lime.
6 Know what the requirements for mortars are.
7 Understand the meaning of cement/aggregate ratio and water/cement ratio and appreciate their importance in the strengths of concretes.

Aggregates are divided into two main groups:

1 *Fine aggregate or sand* which passes through a 5 mm sieve and is used as a filler in concrete and mortar.
2 *Coarse aggregate or shingle* which is coarser than 5 mm and is used as a filler in concrete.

These aggregates may be dug from pits and river beds or sucked up with huge suction pumps or dredged from sand and shingle banks under the sea. They should be free from too much *clay* or *loam* as these consist of very fine particles which increase the surface area of the aggregates. This can be explained by comparing different spherical shapes having similar volumes, such as a football, a number of cricket balls, a greater number of golf balls and a still greater number of marbles. It can be seen that the smaller the particle, then the greater is the surface area for the same volume of material. If the particles are very small then the surface area of these can be enormous in relation to their total volume.

Since the strength of concretes or mortars relies to a great extent on there being sufficient cement paste to cover each particle of aggregate, if the surface area is increased there are likely to be parts which are not covered and can cause a weakness in the concrete or mortar.

Any excess clay impurities will also cause weakness, as they may be present as a coating on the aggregate, and this will break down the bond between the cement and the surface of the stone, thus creating soft and unreliable patches in mortars and concretes.

The aggregates should also be free from *organic impurities*, such as decayed plant life, which may have a harmful effect on the setting action of cement and may also cause discoloration. Aggregates in general should also be hard, durable, contain no soluble particles (that is, anything that will dissolve in water) and be well-graded and free from clay and silt.

Lime

The raw material from which building lime is manufactured is either chalk or limestone. When chalk (or limestone) is burnt at a high temperature it is turned into a product known as *quicklime*. In this form the material is not suitable for use in building, so it is treated by adding water to it; this action is called *slaking*. The quicklime undergoes intense action in the course of which it generates heat and expands, and the water will combine chemically with the quicklime changing it into a *hydrated lime*. It is now an excellent material for building purposes and is ready for use, particularly in mortars and plasters. When the lime is mixed with sand for mortar, water is added to facilitate the mixing, and when this water evaporates the lime is said to have *set*. It then begins to *harden* by slowly changing back into a form of chalk or limestone.

Chalks vary in composition in different parts of the country, ranging from white to grey, each producing a different type of lime which can be broadly placed into one of three main categories:

1 Non-hydraulic (will not set under damp conditions)
2 Semi-hydraulic (will partialy set under damp conditions)
3 Eminently hydraulic (will set under damp conditions)

The non-hydraulic limes are produced from white chalk and these slake rapidly, are very suitable for plastering, and may also be used in mortars for brickwork in which cement is also added.

The semi-hydraulic limes have a slower slaking rate and are suitable for brickwork, and may be used for plastering provided the slaking action is complete.

The third group is produced from grey chalks, has a slow slaking rate, and is very suitable for brickwork and concretes where great strength is not necessary. The setting action of hydraulic limes is caused by the clay-like constituents in the limestone; therefore after being mixed with water they should not be allowed to stand for more than twenty-four hours, otherwise their hydraulic properties will be lost. BS 890 deals with building limes.

Cement

Ordinary Portland cement is made by burning a mixture of chalk (or limestone) and clay, which is then ground down to a very fine powder. The kiln in which it is burnt is called a *rotary kiln*, a large cylinder about 90 metres long and sloping downwards with the heat source at the lower end. A clay-and-chalk slurry is fed in from the upper end. The kiln slowly rotates while the burning is in progress and the slurry is changed into a clinker, which on passing through the kiln is transferred to the ball mill. This is a steel drum, partially filled with steel balls, into which the clinker is fed while the drum is rotating. The clinker is thus ground into so fine a powder that it would pass a sieve which has an aperture width of 90 μm.

BS 12 covers the requirements for Portland cement and deals with the fineness, strength in compression, soundness, setting times and chemical composition.

Mortars

Every mortar should:

Have sufficient strength for the purpose for which it is required. In no case need it be stronger than the brick which will be bedded in the mortar.
Be workable so that the bricklayer can handle it easily.
Have a good bond with the bricks or blocks which are bedded in it.
Be durable and resistant to frost and chemical attack.

For general brickwork a lime mortar using a hydraulic lime and sand, or a mixture of cement, lime and sand, will satisfy all the above requirements, but good general mixes would be as follows:

1 part of hydraulic lime to 3 parts of sand by volume; or
1 part of hydraulic lime to 4 parts of sand by volume; or
1 part of cement, 1 part lime to 6 parts of sand by volume; or
1 part of cement, 2 parts lime to 9 parts of sand by volume.

Another product called *masonry cement* is available on the market and this may be used in the proportion of 1 part cement to 3 parts of sand, or 1 part cement to 4 parts of sand, for general brickwork.

Strong cement/sand mortars are not usually necessary for general brickwork, but these are called for in work requiring high strength or to be done in exposed conditions where engineering bricks would be most likely to be used. The mortar in these cases may be 1 part cement to 3 or 4 parts of sand by volume.

Concrete

This is a mixture of cement and fine and coarse aggregates, with water added to facilitate the mixing, make the mix workable and start the setting action of the cement by causing various chemical ingredients to form different compounds.

The proportion of cement to aggregates by weight is commonly known as the cement/aggregate ratio.

The proportion of water to cement by weight is the water/cement ratio. Both of these ratios play an important part in the strengths of concrete.

Mixes

For general purposes a mix of 1:3:6 is sufficient, but if a stronger concrete is required, then a 1:2:4 mix would be preferred. These ratios, however, must be regarded as only applicable for general concreting purposes, and may not be ideal for high-quality concrete. The amount of water necessary for these concrete mixes would be between 22.7 and 27.24 litres per 50 kg of cement, which should give sufficient workability for tamping by hand. If more water than this were used it would have a serious effect on the ultimate strength of the concrete.

Self-assessment questions

1   Fine aggregate is that which passes a
    (a)   3 mm sieve
    (b)   5 mm sieve
    (c)   7 mm sieve

2   For similar volumes, which aggregate has the greatest surface area?
    (a)   75 mm
    (b)   100 mm
    (c)   150 mm

3   Hydrated lime is produced by
    (a)   grinding limestone
    (b)   burning limestone
    (c)   mixing quicklime with water

4   Slaking is the term used when
    (a)   limestone is burnt
    (b)   burnt limestone is mixed with water
    (c)   burnt limestone is mixed with sand

5   When eminently hydraulic limes are mixed with sand and water for mortars, they should be
    (a)   left for seven days
    (b)   left for fourteen days
    (c)   used the same day

6   Portland cement is made by burning a mixture of
    (a)   limestone and shingle
    (b)   limestone and clay
    (c)   shingle and clay

7   Mortars for general brickwork should have
    (a)   the same strength as the bricks
    (b)   less strength
    (c)   greater strength

8   Explain the meaning of
    (a)   hydrated lime
    (b)   hydraulic lime

9   How is the clinker ground down to a fine powder for cement?

10 State a suitable mortar mix for
    (a)   general brickwork
    (b)   engineering brickwork

Chapter 3

Tools

After reading this chapter you should be able to:

1 Appreciate the importance of obtaining and using the correct tools for the intended work.
2 Carry out adjustments to a spirit level.
3 Splice a line.
4 Understand the terms of various cut bricks.
5 Explain how a left-handed trowel differs from a right-handed trowel.
6 By means of a sketch show a simple method of ensuring that closers are cut to the same size.

Basic tools

The tools a bricklayer uses should be:

Robust.
Capable of withstanding a great deal of use and wear.
Capable of giving many years of service.
Used for the job for which they were intended, and not as a substitute for another tool. It is wrong, for example, to slide a trowel into the joint underneath a freshly laid sill and attempt to lift it by levering it up with the handle of the trowel. The trowel may become bent or even snap in half. A cold chisel should be used for this purpose.

Cheap tools may not be a good buy, and it is generally best to get those which are made by well-known manufacturers who have a reputation for producing good tools. Tools develop a 'character' which is moulded into them by their user, and a good craftsman will take great care of them, because they represent a part of his own character. This can be seen by observing *any good craftsman* – regardless of his craft – and looking at the way in which he handles and takes pride in the tools of his craft. Indeed, many foremen can sum up the character of a new hand by the appearance of his tools.

The tools needed for the general work of a bricklayer are as follows.

Brick trowels are made in sizes ranging from 225 to 350 mm, and although it may be felt that the larger sizes may produce more work, there is no evidence to prove this, and it is found that a 250 or 275 mm blade is suitable for most general work. Trowels are available with left-handed or right-handed blades (Figure 12). A left-handed craftsman should ask for a left-handed blade when buying a trowel.

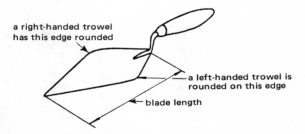

a right-handed trowel has this edge rounded

a left-handed trowel is rounded on this edge

blade length

Figure 12   *Brick trowel*

Pointing trowels generally range in size from 75 to 150 mm; the smaller ones are often referred to as *dotters*, and the larger ones as *bed jointers*.

Club hammers of 0.90 or 1.135 kg are generally heavy enough for cutting bricks or cutting away holes and chases in brickwork (Figure 13).

The *bolster* or *boaster* is used in conjunction with the club hammer for cutting bricks, and

Figure 13   *Club hammer*

Figure 14   *Bolster or boaster*   Figure 15   *Cold chisel*

should always be used for this purpose in preference to a trowel (Figure 14).

The *cold chisel* is also used with a club hammer when cutting holes or chases (Figure 15).

The *brick hammer* or *comb hammer*, of the older type, had heads which consisted of a hammer at one end and a blade at the other. But the modern type has, instead of the blade, a slotted end into which a blade or comb is inserted. The comb hammer is slotted at both ends of the head so that a comb may be inserted in one end and a blade in the other. No sharpening of blades is necessary, the worn blade being changed for a new one, as the blades and combs can be purchased quite cheaply (Figure 16).

All these types of hammer are used for trimming the bricks after they have been cut with a hammer and bolster.

Spirit levels are available in various lengths ranging from about 225 mm to 1.2 m. The shorter lengths are used for adjusting small work or individual bricks whereas the longer levels are used for plumbing the angles of work vertically and levelling the courses horizontally. Levels are available with fixed or adjustable bubble tubes; the latter is preferable because if the level is inaccurate it is quite a simple matter to readjust the bubble (Figure 17).

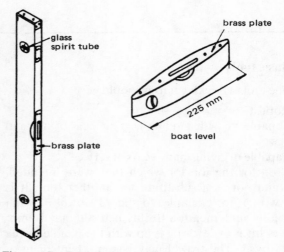

Figure 17   *Spirit level*

The *plumb rule* is not used so often today, but it is an excellent tool and has the virtue of being always accurate and needing no adjustment. The *plumb-bob* is usually of lead, weighing about 2 kg (Figure 18).

The *rule* is usually of boxwood. The 600 mm four-fold rule is generally the most convenient as this fits in the pocket quite easily, although some craftsmen prefer the 1 m rule. An alternative type is a 2 m steel tape which rolls into a small steel container, has the advantage of being invaluable for measurements needed in confined enclosures, and is easily carried in the pocket.

The *hawk* is generally made out of a piece of timber 200 mm^2 (or a piece of resin-bonded

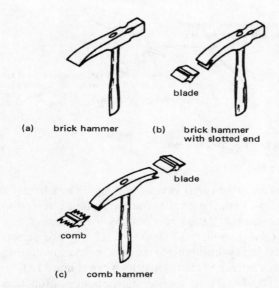

Figure 16   *Types of hammers*

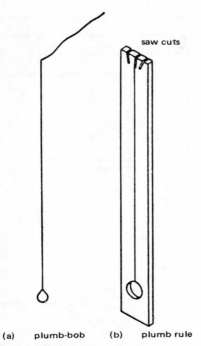

saw cuts

(a)   plumb-bob   (b)   plumb rule

Figure 18   *A plumb-bob and rule*

Figure 19   *A hawk*

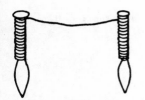

Figure 20   *Line and pins*

Figure 21   *Brick jointer*

the *line* in 'knots'. For general purposes two knots of line are sufficient on one pair of pins (Figure 20).

Brick jointers are from 60 to 125 mm long and are used for forming recessed joints (Figure 21).

The *pointing rule* is a light, wooden straight-edge usually 1 m long, 50 by 6 mm thick in section, with two corks or distance pieces fixed on the back to allow the pointing mortar-droppings to fall through (Figure 22).

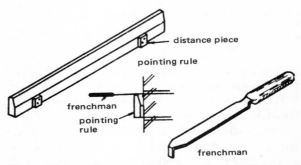

distance piece

pointing rule

frenchman

pointing rule

frenchman

Figure 22   *Application of pointing rule and frenchman*

The *frenchman* is not generally purchased but is usually made from an old table knife. The end of the knife is heated, and with a hammer and chisel is cut back about 25 mm on each side of the end. Then the end is re-heated and bent over about 9 mm from the end. Refer to Figure 23.

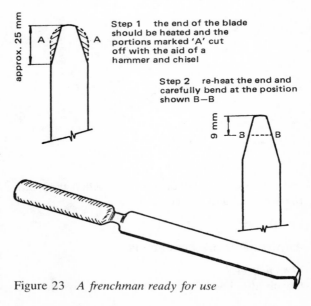

approx. 25 mm

A   A

Step 1   the end of the blade should be heated and the portions marked 'A' cut off with the aid of a hammer and chisel

Step 2   re-heat the end and carefully bend at the position shown B—B

9 mm

B ------ B

plywood would serve the purpose admirably) with a handle fixed underneath, and is used for carrying the mortar when you are pointing (Figure 19). Aluminium hawks are also available; these are lightweight and convenient for handling.

Pins, made of steel, are purchased in pairs, and

Figure 23   *A frenchman ready for use*

Note: Do not attempt to bend cold as the blade is liable to snap!

The *jointing iron* is usually made from an old bucket handle or piece of mild steel rod, as shown in Figure 24.

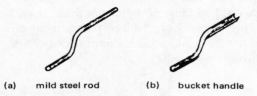

(a)   mild steel rod   (b)   bucket handle

Figure 24   *Jointing irons*

The *soft brush* is for cleaning down the face work when completed.

The *laying-on trowel* is for rendering or laying floor screeds (Figure 25).

The *closer* and *bat gauges* are easily made and are very useful for marking off bats and closers and keeping them all even in size (Figure 26).

Figure 25   *Laying-on trowel*

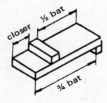

Figure 26   *Closer gauge*

There are many other tools for special work but these are beyond the scope of this book.

Adjustment and care of tools

The spirit level

Check the level by putting two screws into a

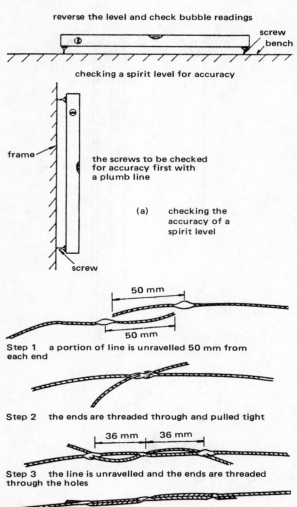

reverse the level and check bubble readings

checking a spirit level for accuracy

frame

the screws to be checked for accuracy first with a plumb line

screw

(a)   checking the accuracy of a spirit level

50 mm

50 mm

Step 1   a portion of line is unravelled 50 mm from each end

Step 2   the ends are threaded through and pulled tight

36 mm   36 mm

Step 3   the line is unravelled and the ends are threaded through the holes

Step 4   the line is pulled tight and the ends cut off

(b)   repairing lines

Figure 27

board or bench equal to the length of the level apart, and turn one of the screws down until the bubble settles between the lines marked on the glass tube when the level is placed across the screws. Then reverse the spirit level and replace it on the screws. If the bubble is in between the lines the level is accurate. If an eror is noticed correct half of it by adjusting one of the screws and the other half by adjusting the spirit tube in the level.

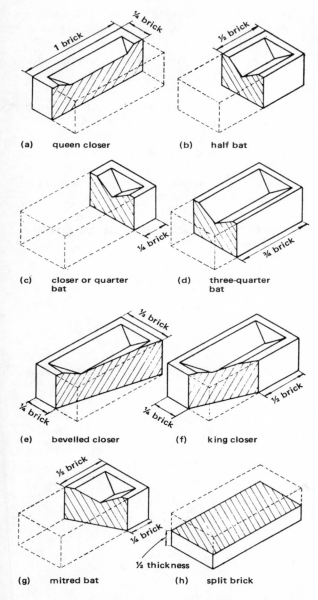

(a) queen closer (b) half bat

(c) closer or quarter bat (d) three-quarter bat

(e) bevelled closer (f) king closer

(g) mitred bat (h) split brick

Figure 28 *Various shapes which can be cut from bricks*

Lines

If a broken line is repaired by tying a knot then the line is likely to be held away from the wall by the body of the knot: it is therefore better to splice the line. A method for this is as follows (see Figure 27(b)):

1 Unravel a small portion of the line and form a small hole about 50 mm away from each end. Thread the ends of the line into each hole.
2 Pull the ends of the line tight so that the unravelled portions come together.
3 Unravel another small hole about 36 mm away from the connection on each side and thread in the loose end.
4 Cut off any surplus line.

When repairing nylon lines they may be spliced in a similar way but, as the ends of the line tend to fray, they should be sealed by heating with a cigarette end or gently heating with a match.

Trowels

Wash trowels well at the end of a day's work; an oily rag will keep them in good condition and safeguard them from rust.

Brick-cutting

Bricks are often cut in various shapes to suit bonding requirements. A sharp blow with a trowel will often snap a brick, but this method is not recommended. It is far better to use a hammer and bolster, which will produce a more accurate and a much cleaner cut – it also causes less wear and tear on the trowel.

Figure 28 shows some shapes which can be cut from bricks.

Re-check by reversing the level as before.

You can check the vertical bubbles in a similar way by fixing two screws into an upright piece of timber, and check it for accuracy with a plumb-bob before adjusting the spirit level (Figure 27(a)).

Self-assessment questions

1 The most suitable tool for easing a heavy pre-cast lintel on its mortar bed over an opening is a
  (a) brick trowel
  (b) club hammer
  (c) cold chisel

2   A pointing rule is a
    (a)   light wooden straightedge
    (b)   recognized procedure for pointing brickwork
    (c)   method of keeping all the perpends even

3   When a line becomes broken it is best to
    (a)   splice the two ends
    (b)   tie them in a knot
    (c)   throw away the shorter length and use the longer one

4   A queen closer is a brick which is
    (a)   a half-brick wide at one end and a quarter-brick at the other through its length
    (b)   a half-brick wide at one side and a quarter-brick wide at the other across its width
    (c)   a quarter-brick wide at both ends through the length of the brick

5   Make a neat sketch showing a suitable gauge for the marking and cutting of closers.

6   Make a sketch of a mitred bat.

7   Describe the method of making a frenchman for pointing.

8   Describe two types of jointers for pointing brickwork.

Chapter 4

Brickwork bonds

After reading this chapter you should be able to:

1 Have a good understanding of the principles of bonding of brickwork.

2 Appreciate the importance of bonding brickwork.

3 Understand the arrangement of bricks in various types of bond.

4 Set out quoins, stopped ends and junction walls in various bonding patterns.

Bonding

This is the term given to the various recognized arrangements of brickwork in walling.

These bond patterns are essential for any wall which is intended to carry heavy loads and they prevent, as far as possible, any structural failure. For this to be effective the bonding must distribute the loading evenly throughout the length of the wall, so that each part of the wall carries a small amount of the load (Figure 29). If, on the other hand, the load is not distributed but localized to certain portions of the wall, then this may cause uneven settlement and cracking (Figure 30).

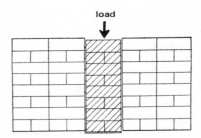

Figure 30 *Uneven load distribution due to poor bonding*
The shaded area of the walling takes all the load and has a tendency towards more settlement than the rest of the wall

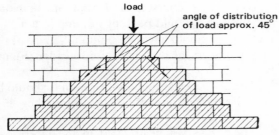

Figure 29 *Even load distribution due to good bonding*
The shaded area shows how the load is distributed over a large area of walling

In addition to the even distribution of loads throughout the wall, stability is also achieved by correct bonding at corners, attached piers, junction and separating walls, and ensuring that they are well *tied in together*.

A simple example of this is demonstrated in the stabilizing of cardboard strips such as those which are used for egg-packing cases, or a certain type of hollow plasterboard partition where the two faces are held quite rigidly together by means of cardboard spacers *bonded* together.

The bonding of brickwork, however, is not confined wholly to strength requirements. Very often a certain bond is introduced for its pleasing appearance, or another bond to make decorative patterns is incorporated in walling facework. In this way a huge flank wall which may otherwise be just a drab piece of walling may be transformed into quite an interesting architectural feature.

In addition to strength and appearance, economy may also play an important part in the selection of a facing bond, as the number of facing bricks per 0.84 m² will vary according to the bond used. Table 5 gives the approximate number of bricks required per 0.84 m² in various bonds using bricks of different depths or thickness.

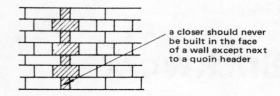

Figure 32   *An example of bad bonding*

Table 5   *The approximate number of facing bricks required per 0.84 m² of walling in various bonds*

Type of bond	Thickness of brick		
	50 mm	*65 mm*	*70 mm*
English bond	90	72	66
Dutch bond	90	72	66
Flemish bond	80	64	59
English garden-wall bond	75	60	55
Flemish garden-wall bond	69	56	51
Stretcher bond	60	48	44
Header bond	120	96	88

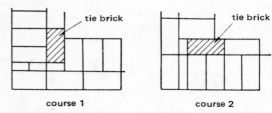

Figure 33   *Plans showing the tie brick bonding the walls together*

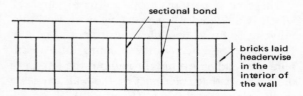

Figure 34   *Plan of a 2-brick thick wall*

Certain general principles may be applied to bonding:

1   The correct lap should be set out and maintained by the introduction of:
    (a)   a closer next to the quoin header (Figure 31(a)); or
    (b)   a three-quarter bat starting the stretcher course (Figure 31(b)).

2   The perpends or cross-joints in alternate courses should be kept vertical (Figure 31(a)).
3   There should be no *straight joints* in a wall, that is, no vertical joints should coincide in consecutive courses, or, if they are unavoidable, they should be kept to a minimum.
4   Closers should never be built in the face of the wall except next to the quoin header (Figure 32).
5   The *tie bricks* at junctions or quoins should be well-bonded to secure the walls together (Figure 33).
6   The bricks which are laid in the interior of thick walls should be laid headerwise as far as possible (Figure 34).
7   *Sectional bond* should be maintained across the wall, that is, the bond on the back should be in line with the bond on the face side of the wall (Figure 34).

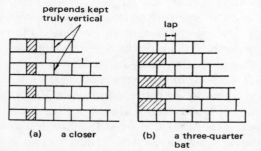

Figure 31   *The bond formed by a closer and a three-quarter bat*

8   To achieve the maximum strength in a wall, all the joints in the interior of the wall should be kept filled or *flushed in* with mortar in every course. You can do this by mixing a quantity of mortar to a grout or slurry and running it into the joints between the bricks which have been laid in the wall.

Figure 35   *Stretcher bond*

Types of bond

There is an infinite number of possible bonding arrangements, but the following are some of the more common ones in general use.

Stretcher bond consists of all bricks laid as stretchers on every course with the courses laid half-bond to each other; this is effected in a plain wall with stopped ends by introducing a half-bat as the starting brick to alternate courses. Usually only used in walls of a half-brick in thickness (Figure 35).

Header bond is satisfactory for walls one brick thick and consists of all headers, with the bond being formed by three-quarter bats at the quoin, and is generally used in footing courses or walling curved on plan (Figure 36).

English bond has alternate courses of headers and stretchers, with a closer placed next to the quoin header to form the lap. There is, however, a variation where a closer is not used in the header course, and the lap is formed by starting each stretcher course with a three-quarter bat. Such variation is not very common but occasionally instructions are given on a site that no closers are to be used in the face work (Figure 37).

Flemish bond consists of alternate headers and stretchers with the headers in one course being placed centrally over the stretcher in the course below. A closer is placed next to the quoin header to form the lap (Figure 38).

Dutch bond is somewhat similar to English bond in that it consists of alternate header and stretcher courses, but there are no closers in the header course, and the bond is formed by starting each stretcher course with a three-quarter bat. In addition the stretcher courses are laid half-bond to each other; this is effected by placing a header on *alternate stretcher* courses next to the three-quarter bat. The perpends in this bond follow

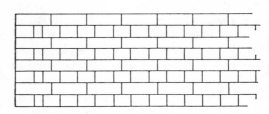

Figure 36   *Header bond*

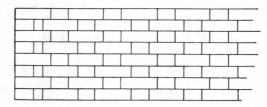

Figure 37   *English bond*

Figure 38   *Flemish bond*

each other diagonally across the wall in an unbroken line (Figure 39).

English garden-wall bond, sometimes called *Sussex bond*, consists of three or sometimes five courses of stretchers to one course of headers: the stretcher courses being laid half-bond to each other (Figure 40(a) and (b)).

Flemish garden-wall bond consists of three or

sometimes five stretchers to one header in each course. The header in one course is laid centrally over the middle stretcher in the course immediately below (Figure 41(a), (b) and (c)).

Although garden-wall bonds are occasionally used as face bonds, their main use is in 1-brick thick walls where a face side of neat brickwork is required on both sides of the wall. The varying brick lengths make it difficult to keep a fair face on both sides of the wall unless the number of headers is greatly reduced. If the strength of the wall is of secondary importance, then the number of stretcher courses to each header course in English garden-wall bond may be increased to five instead of three (Figure 40(b)). Similarly, in Flemish garden-wall bond, the number of stretchers to one header in each course may be increased to five (Figure 41(c)).

Monk bond usually consists of two stretchers to one header in each course. The header is laid centrally over the cross-joint between two stretchers in the course below (Figure 42(a), (b), (c) and (d)). This bond can be made to have a very pleasing appearance by *blinding out* the joint between the stretchers with a coloured mortar matching the colour of the bricks, thus making the two bricks appear as a 450 mm stretcher, giving an elongated-type of Flemish bond (sometimes referred to as *flying Flemish bond*). It is particularly effective on long lengths of walling because of the apparent reduction in the number of cross-joints in the face of the wall (Figure 42(b)).

Rat-trap bond is used where strength is not of vital importance, because this is a brick-on-edge bond with the middle of the wall being left hollow. It is generally used for garden walls, or walls of buildings which are being tile-hung, or have

some other similar treatment on the face.

There are two variations: (1) where the stretchers and headers are laid alternately (Figure 43) or (2) with three stretchers to one header.

(a) using three stretchers to one header

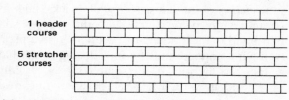

(b) using five stretchers to one header

Figure 40 *English garden-wall bonds*

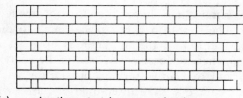

(a) using three stretchers to one header

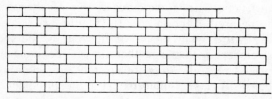

(b) bonding from the quoin

(c) using five stretchers to one header

Figure 41 *Flemish garden-wall bonds*

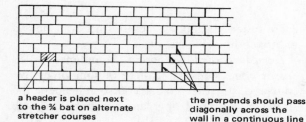

a header is placed next to the ¾ bat on alternate stretcher courses

the perpends should pass diagonally across the wall in a continuous line

Figure 39 *Dutch bond*

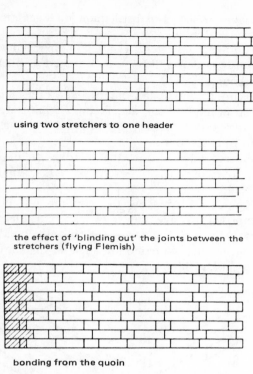

(a)   using two stretchers to one header

(b)   the effect of 'blinding out' the joints between the stretchers (flying Flemish)

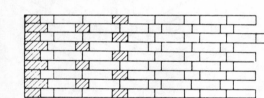

(c)   bonding from the quoin

(d)   bonding from the quoin

Figure 42   *Monk bonds*

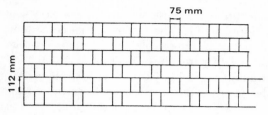

(a)   elevation of a wall built in rat-trap bond

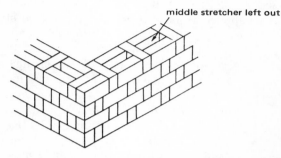

middle stretcher left out

(b)   isometric view of a quoin built in rat-trap bond

Figure 43   *Rat-trap headers and stretchers laid alternately*

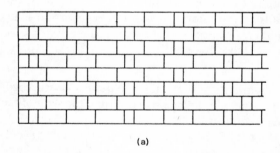

(a)

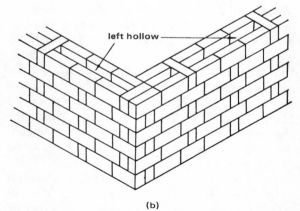

left hollow

(b)

Figure 44   *Rat-trap bond using three stretchers to one header*

The bond is formed at a stopped end or reveal by laying two headers together (Figure 44).

Miscellaneous bonds are formed to suit the individual requirements of a designer. Sometimes they may be standard bonds with coloured bricks or projecting headers being introduced to form patterns. In other types, *travelling headers* pass diagonally across the wall in continuous lines. There is an infinite variety of these bonds and they are interesting to use.

Setting out bonds

You have just been shown the standard patterns

of various bonds, but in some cases it may be difficult to apply these to quoins, junction walls and stopped ends. The reason is that consistency of bonding is impossible to maintain. For example, when setting out English and Dutch bonds for walls of 1 and 2 bricks in thickness, the pattern is the same on both faces, whereas on 1½- and 2½-brick walls the pattern is different. That is, headers on one face and stretchers on the other.

So any rules concerning bonding in general can only be applied *as far as is practicable*. A general rule for quoins, stopped ends and junction walls in English and Dutch bonds is that where a wall changes direction, so the bond will also change, that is, if there are stretchers on one face then the adjoining face will be headers. This, however, cannot be applied in every case. In many cases, as in a 1½-brick junction wall adjoining a 2-brick main wall or with quoins having uneven walls, such as 1½ and 2 bricks in thickness, there must be two adjoining faces having similar bonds.

One rule, however, should always be applied. When setting out quoins or junction walls, care should be taken to ensure correct *tying in* of the walls at the internal angles to achieve the maximum resistance against cracking due to shrinkage or uneven settlement.

Quoins

The bonding arrangements to quoins vary according to the bonds which are used and the sizes of the walls comprising the corners.

Figure 45 shows a quoin built in stretcher bond.

Figure 46 illustrates a quoin built in header bond which is not a usual bond for general walling being more commonly used for walls curved on plan. Figures 47–49 show quoins for 1-, 1½- and 2-brick walls built in English bond. Figures 50–52 illustrate quoins built in Flemish bond. Note the use of three-quarter bats to form the bond. Figures 53–55 show the bonding arrangements for 1-, 1½-, and 2-brick walls in Dutch bond. Note that the courses in Dutch bond go in sets of four. Figure 56 illustrates a 1-brick wall built in English garden-wall bond.

Figure 57 shows a 1½-brick wall faced in English garden-wall bond and backed with English bond. This illustrates how differing bonds may be used in conjunction with each other. Note once again that the courses are also in sets of four.

Figure 58 shows a 1-brick quoin built in Flemish garden-wall bond.

Figure 59 indicates a 1½-brick quoin faced with Flemish garden-wall bond and backed with English bond.

Figure 60 shows an isometric view of a 1-brick quoin in monk bond, and Figure 61 illustrates a 1½-brick quoin faced in monk bond and backed with English bond.

Figures 62–63 show the bonding to quoins comprised of walls of uneven thickness in English bond.

Figures 64–65 show the bonding to quoins comprised of unequal thicknesses in Flemish bond. Similarly, Figures 66–68 show the bonding arrangements to quoins of unequal thicknessed walls in Dutch bond.

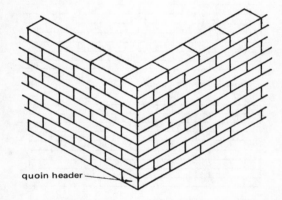

Figure 45   *A quoin in a ½-brick wall in stretcher bond*

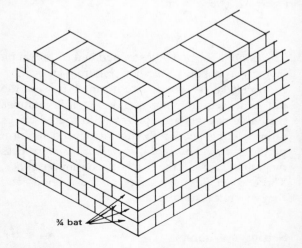

Figure 46   *A quoin in a 1-brick wall built in header bond*

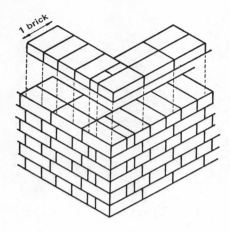

Figure 47 *An isometric view of a 1-brick quoin in English bond with the top course raised to show the bonding to alternate courses*

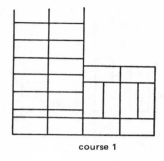

course 1

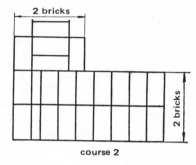

2 bricks

2 bricks

course 2

Figure 49 *Plans showing the bonding of alternate courses of a 2-brick quoin in English bond*

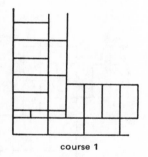

course 1

Figure 48 *Plans showing the bonding of alternate courses of a 1½-brick quoin in English bond*

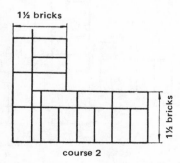

1½ bricks

1½ bricks

course 2

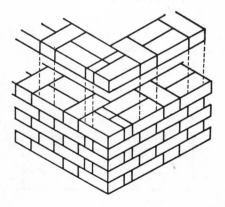

Figure 50 *An isometric view of a 1-brick quoin in Flemish bond with the top course raised to show the bonding to alternate courses*

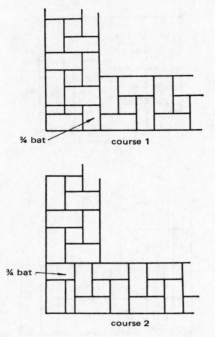

¾ bat   **course 1**

¾ bat

course 2

Figure 51   *Plans showing the bonding of alternate courses of a 1½-brick quoin in Flemish bond*

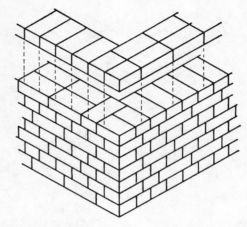

Figure 53   *An isometric view of a 1-brick quoin in Dutch bond with the top course raised to show the bonding to alternate courses*

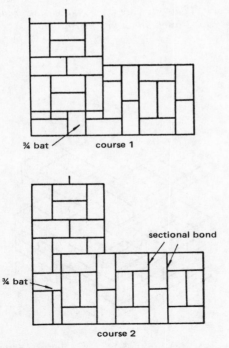

¾ bat   **course 1**

sectional bond

¾ bat

course 2

Figure 52   *Plans showing the bonding of alternate courses of a 2-brick quoin in Flemish bond*

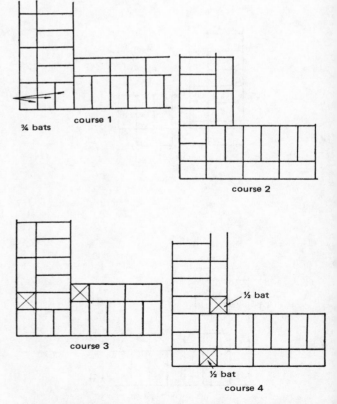

¾ bats   **course 1**

course 2

course 3

½ bat

½ bat

course 4

Figure 54   *Plans showing the bonding arrangement of each set of four courses for a 1½-brick quoin in Dutch bond*

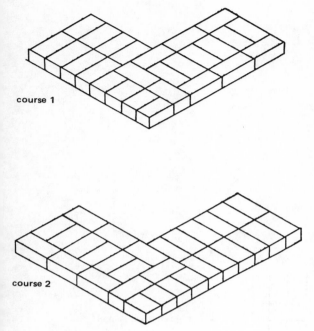

course 1

course 2

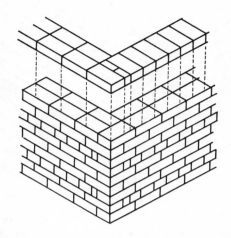

Figure 56   *An isometric view of a 1-brick quoin in English garden-wall bond with the bond raised to show the bonding to alternate courses*

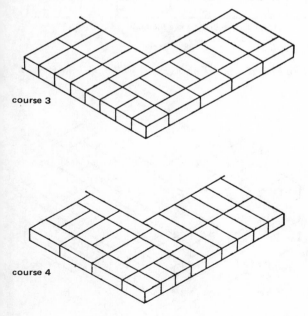

course 3

course 4

Figure 55   *Isometric views showing the bonding arrangement of each set of four courses for a 2-brick quoin in Dutch bond*

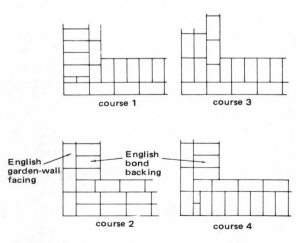

course 1

course 3

English garden-wall facing

English bond backing

course 2

course 4

Figure 57   *Plans showing the bonding arrangement of a quoin faced with English garden-wall bond and backed with English bond*

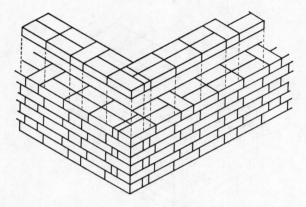

Figure 58   *An isometric view of a 1-brick quoin in Flemish garden-wall bond with the top course raised to show the bonding to alternate courses*

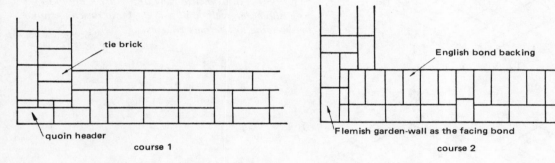

tie brick

quoin header

course 1

English bond backing

Flemish garden-wall as the facing bond

course 2

Figure 59   *Plans showing the bonding arrangement of a quoin faced with Flemish garden-wall bond and backed with English bond*

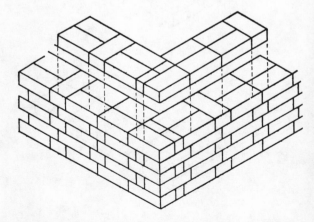

Figure 60   *An isometric view of a 1-brick quoin in monk bond with the top course raised to show the bonding to alternate courses*

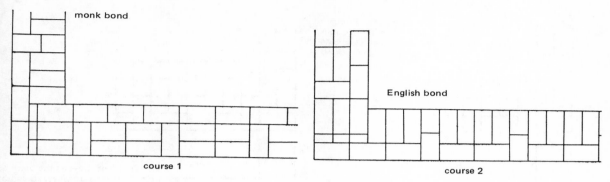

Figure 61   *Plans showing the bonding of alternate courses of a 1½-brick quoin, with monk bond on the face side and English bond on the back*

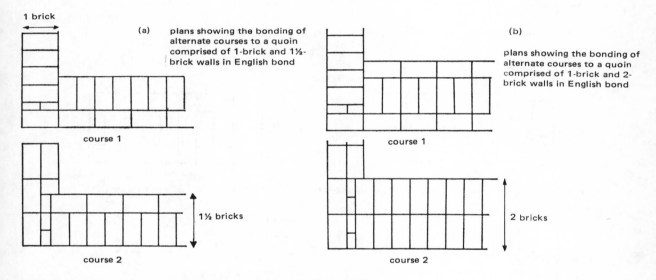

Figure 62   *Bonding of quoins to walls of uneven thickness in English bond*

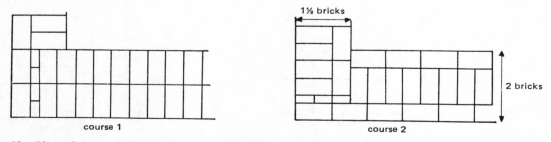

Figure 63   *Plans showing the bonding of alternate courses to a quoin comprised of 1½-brick and 2-brick walls in English bond*

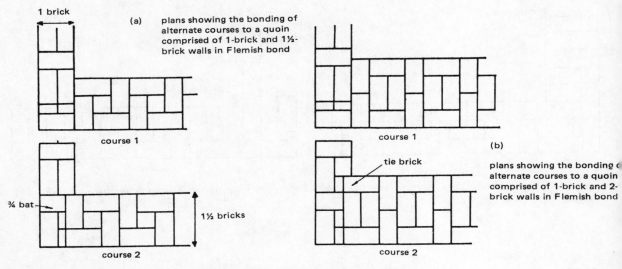

Figure 64   *Bonding of quoins to walls of uneven thickness in Flemish bond*

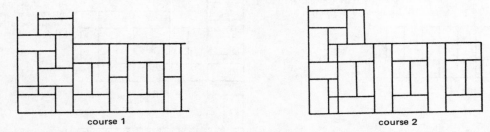

Figure 65   *Plans showing the bonding of alternate courses to a quoin comprised of 1½-brick and 2-brick walls in Flemish bond*

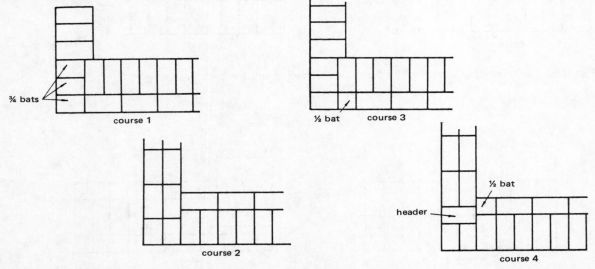

Figure 66   *Plans showing the bonding of each set of four courses to a quoin comprised of 1-brick and 1½-brick walls in Dutch bond*

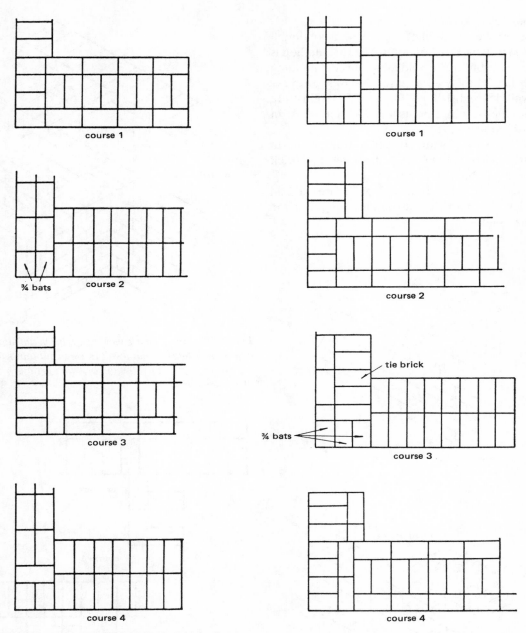

course 1

course 2

¾ bats

course 3

course 4

course 1

course 2

tie brick

¾ bats

course 3

course 4

Figure 67 *Plans showing the bonding of each set of four courses to a quoin comprised of 1-brick and 2-brick walls in Dutch bond*

Figure 68 *Plans showing the bonding of each set of four courses to a quoin comprised of 1½-brick and 2-brick walls in Dutch bond*

Junction walls

Figure 69 shows alternate methods of bonding a junction wall in stretcher bond. The first method is the simplest but the second maintains the bonding on the face of the wall. Figures 70–74 show junction walls in English bond. Figures 75–79 illustrate the bonding arrangements for junction walls in Flemish bond.

Figures 80–84 show junction walls built in Dutch bond and Figure 85 illustrates a 1-brick junction wall built in monk bond.

Note in all cases how the walls are tied in together to obtain the maximum strength at the internal angles.

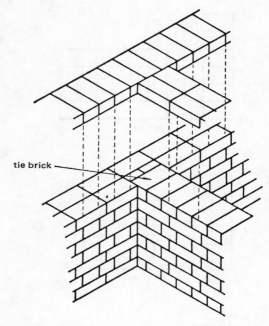

Figure 70   *An isometric view of a 1-brick junction wall adjoining a 1-brick main wall in English bond with the top course raised to show the bonding arrangement in alternate courses*

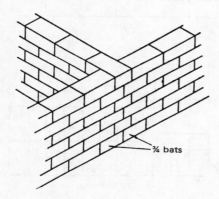

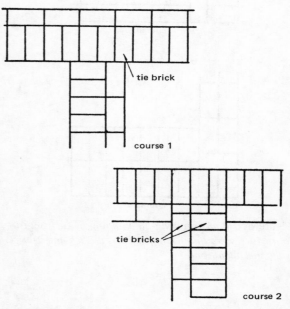

Figure 71   *Plans showing the bonding arrangement for alternate courses in a 1½-brick junction wall in English bond*

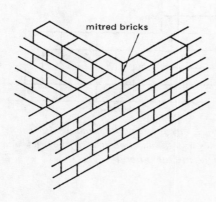

Figure 69   *Alternative methods of bonding a junction wall in stretcher bond*

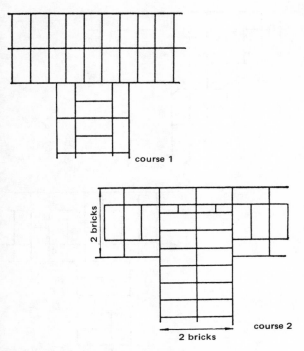

Figure 72   *Plans showing the bonding arrangement of alternate courses for a 2-brick junction wall in English bond*

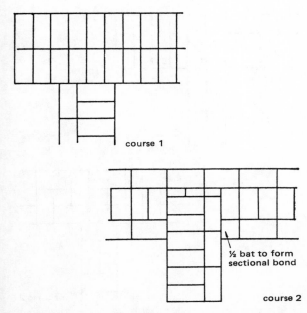

Figure 73   *Plans of alternate courses of a 1½-brick junction wall into a 2-brick main wall in English bond*

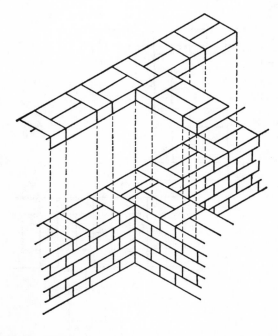

Figure 74   *Plans of alternate courses of a 1-brick junction wall into a 1½-brick main wall in English bond*

Figure 75   *An isometric view of a 1-brick junction wall adjoining a 1-brick wall in Flemish bond, with the top course raised to show the bonding arrangements in alternate courses*

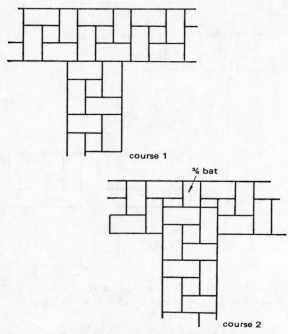

Figure 76   *Plans showing the bonding arrangement for alternate courses in a 1½-brick junction wall in Flemish bond*

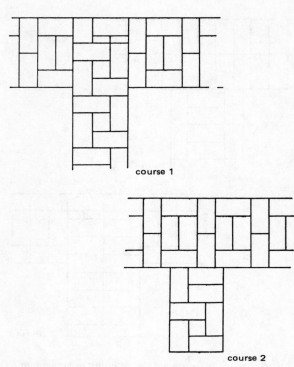

Figure 78   *Plans of alternate courses of a 1½-brick junction wall into a 2-brick main wall in Flemish bond*

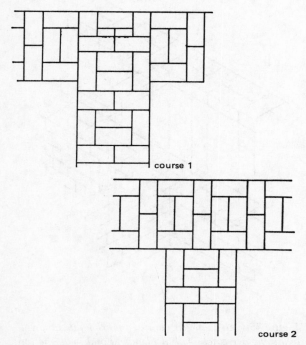

Figure 77   *Plans showing the bonding arrangement for alternate courses in a 2-brick junction wall in Flemish bond*

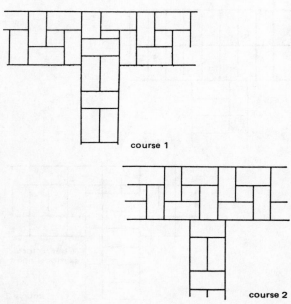

Figure 79   *Plans of alternate courses of a 1-brick junction wall into a 1½-brick main wall in Flemish bond*

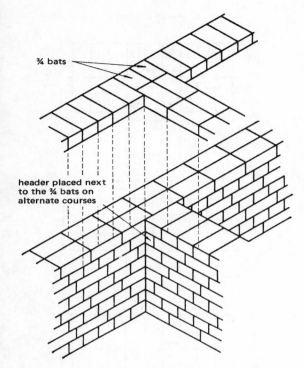

¾ bats

header placed next
to the ¾ bats on
alternate courses

Figure 80 *An isometric view of a 1-brick junction wall adjoining a 1-brick wall in Dutch bond, with the top course raised to show the bonding arrangements in alternate courses*

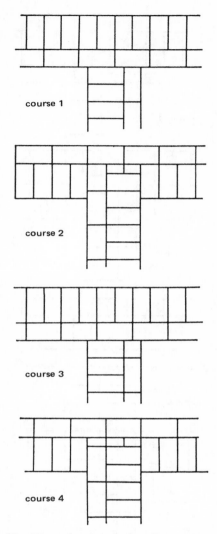

course 1

course 2

course 3

course 4

Figure 81 *Plans showing the bonding arrangement of each set of four courses in a 1½-brick junction wall in Dutch bond*

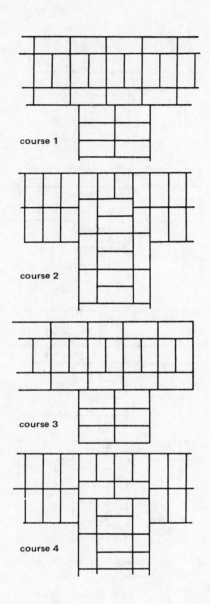

course 1

course 2

course 3

course 4

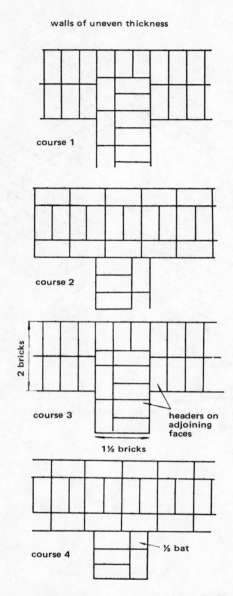

walls of uneven thickness

course 1

course 2

2 bricks

course 3

headers on
adjoining
faces

1½ bricks

course 4

½ bat

Figure 82 *Plans showing the bonding arrangements of each set of four courses in a 2-brick junction wall*

Figure 83 *Plans of each set of four courses of a 1½-brick junction wall into a 2-brick main wall in Dutch bond*

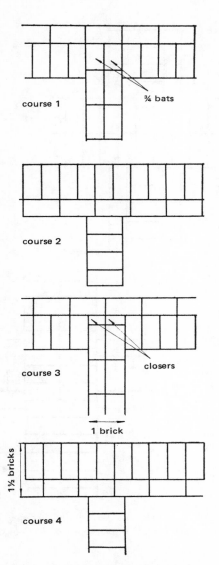

course 1

¾ bats

course 2

course 3

closers

1 brick

1½ bricks

course 4

Figure 84 *Plans of each set of four courses of a 1-brick junction wall into a 1½-brick main wall in Dutch bond*

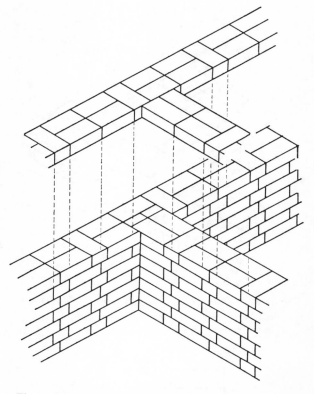

Figure 85 *An isometric view of a 1-brick junction wall adjoining a 1-brick main wall in monk bond, with the top course raised to show the bonding arrangement in alternate courses*

Cross-walls

An isometric view of a 1-brick cross-wall built in English bond is shown in Figure 86, and Figures 87–91 show cross-walls with walls of equal and unequal thickness in English bond.

The general bonding arrangement for a 1-brick cross-wall in Flemish bond is shown in the isometric view in Figure 92. Figures 93–97 show other examples of bonding cross-walls in Flemish bond.

Figures 98–102 show cross-walls of various sizes built in Dutch bond.

The bonding arrangement for a 1-brick cross-wall built in monk bond is shown in Figure 103.

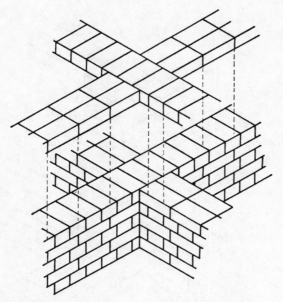

Figure 86   *An isometric view of a 1-brick cross-wall in English bond, with the top course raised to show the bonding arrangements to alternate courses*

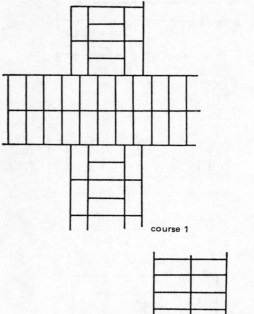

course 1

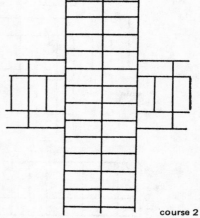

course 2

Figure 88   *Plans showing the bonding arrangements of alternate courses of a 2-brick cross-wall in English bond*

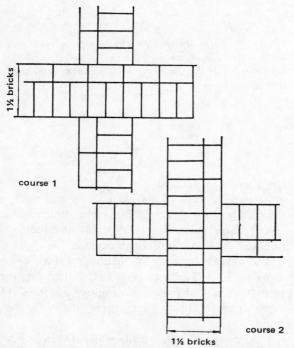

1½ bricks

course 1

1½ bricks

course 2

Figure 87   *Plans showing the bonding arrangements of alternate courses of a 1½-brick cross-wall in English bond*

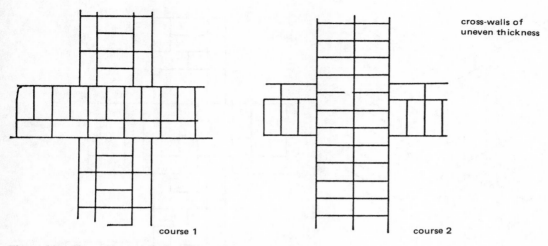

Figure 89   *Plans showing the bonding arrangements of alternate courses of a 2-brick wall crossing a 1½-brick wall in English bond*

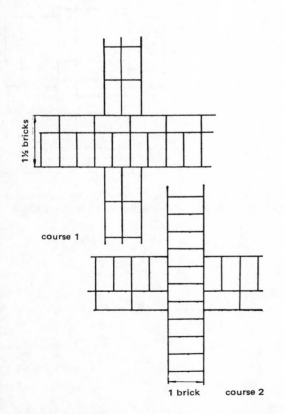

Figure 90   *Plans showing the bonding arrangements for alternate courses of a 1-brick wall crossing a 1½-brick wall in English bond*

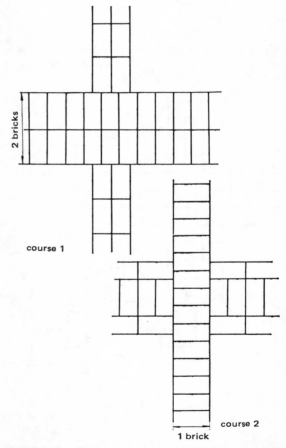

Figure 91   *Plans showing the bonding arrangements for alternate courses of a 1-brick wall crossing a 2-brick wall in English bond*

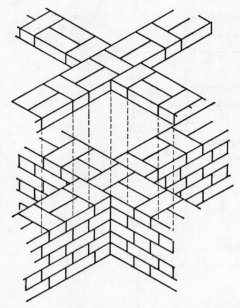

Figure 92   *An isometric view of a 1-brick cross-wall in Flemish bond with the top course raised to show the bonding arrangements to alternate courses*

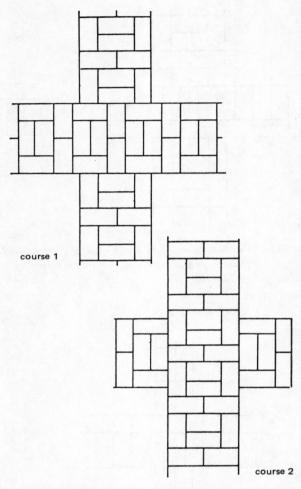

Figure 94   *Plans showing the bonding arrangements of alternate courses of a 2-brick cross-wall in Flemish bond*

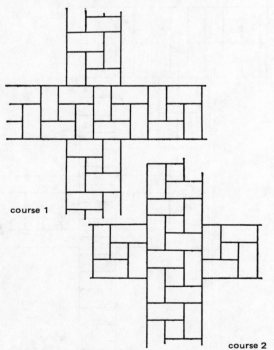

Figure 93   *Plans showing the bonding arrangements of alternate courses of a 1½-brick cross-wall in Flemish bond*

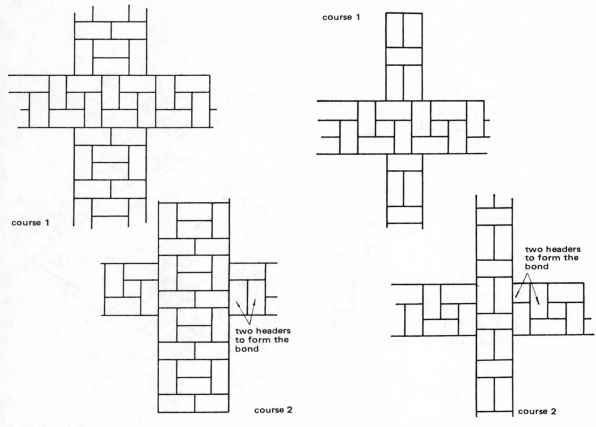

course 1

course 1

two headers
to form the
bond

course 2

two headers
to form the
bond

course 2

Figure 95 *Plans showing the bonding arrangements of alternate courses of a 2-brick wall crossing a 1½-brick wall in Flemish bond*

Figure 96 *Plans showing the bonding arrangements for alternate courses of a 1-brick wall crossing a 1½-brick wall in Flemish bond*

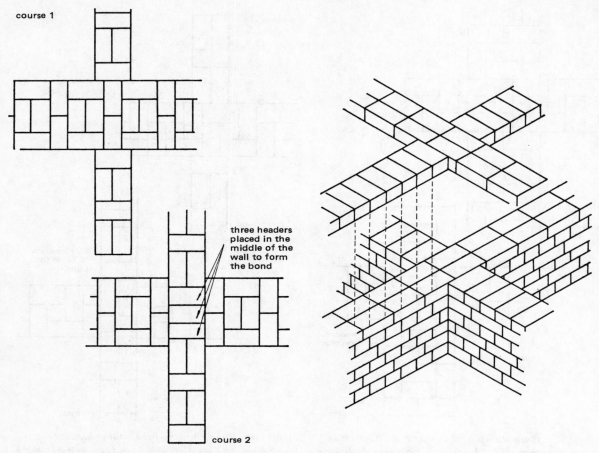

course 1

three headers
placed in the
middle of the
wall to form
the bond

course 2

Figure 97 *Plans showing the bonding arrangements for alternate courses of a 1-brick wall crossing a 2-brick wall in Flemish bond*

Figure 98 *An isometric view of a 1-brick cross-wall in Dutch bond with the top course raised to show the bonding arrangements to each set of four courses*

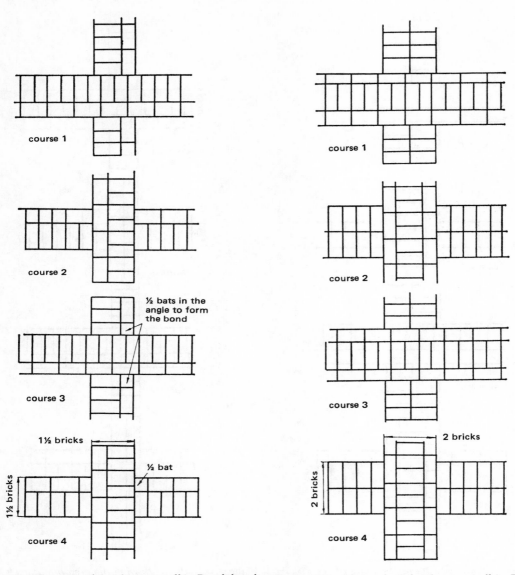

course 1

course 2

½ bats in the
angle to form
the bond

course 3

1½ bricks

½ bat

1½ bricks

course 4

course 1

course 2

course 3

2 bricks

2 bricks

course 4

Figure 99 *Plans of a 1½-brick cross-wall in Dutch bond showing the bonding to each set of four courses*

Figure 100 *Plans of a 2-brick cross-wall in Dutch bond showing the bonding to each set of four courses*

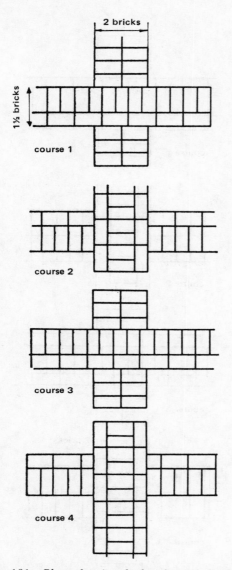

Figure 101 *Plans showing the bonding of each set of four courses of a 2-brick wall crossing a 1½-brick wall in Dutch bond*

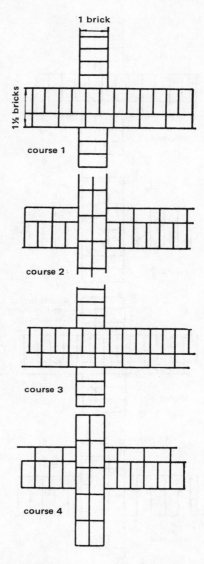

Figure 102 *Plans showing the bonding of each set of four courses of a 1-brick wall crossing a 1½-brick wall in Dutch bond*

Stopped ends

Figures 104–106 show how stopped ends are bonded in English bond. Alternative methods of bonding are shown in the 1½-brick and 2-brick walls because in some cases the stopped end may not be visible, as in the case where a door frame occurs at the front part of the stopped end and the interior face of the reveal is plastered. Since there would be no difference in the strength of the walls, for the sake of economy it would be an advantage not to have the three-quarter bats at the stopped end. One the other hand, if the stop-

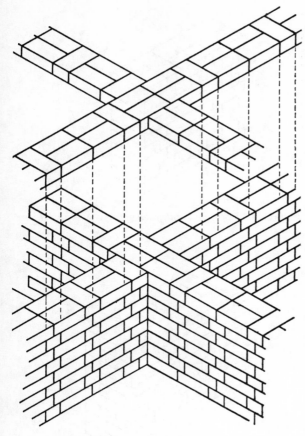

Figure 103 *An isometric view of a 1-brick cross-wall in monk bond, with the top course raised to show the bonding arrangements of alternate courses*

ped end will be visible it is better to show English bond on the stopped end as far as possible. Figures 107–109 show stopped ends in Flemish bond, and Figures 110–112 show stopped ends in Dutch bond.

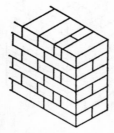

Figure 104 *Stopped end for a 1-brick wall in English bond*

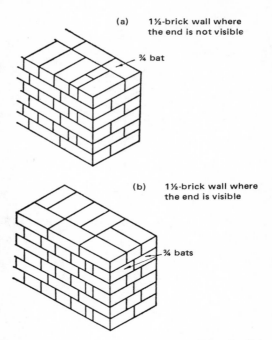

(a) 1½-brick wall where the end is not visible

¾ bat

(b) 1½-brick wall where the end is visible

¾ bats

Figure 105 *Stopped ends for 1½-brick walls in English bond*

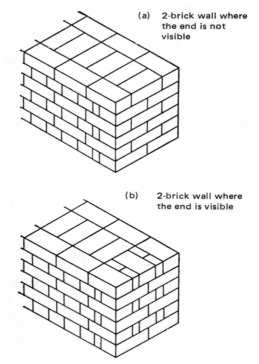

(a) 2-brick wall where the end is not visible

(b) 2-brick wall where the end is visible

Figure 106 *Stopped ends for 2-brick walls in English bond*

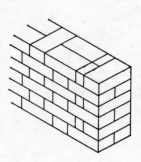

Figure 107   *Stopped end for a 1-brick wall in Flemish bond*

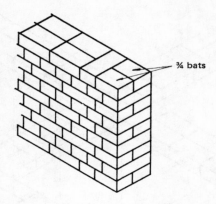

Figure 110   *Stopped end for a 1-brick wall in Dutch bond*

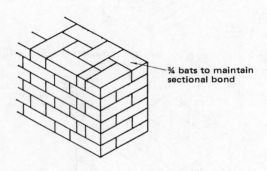

Figure 108   *Stopped end for a 1½-brick wall in Flemish bond*

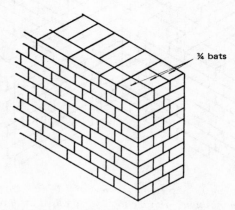

Figure 111   *Stopped end for a 1½-brick wall in Dutch bond*

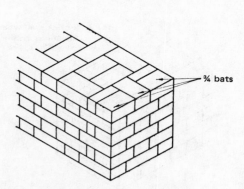

Figure 109   *Stopped end for a 2-brick wall in Flemish bond*

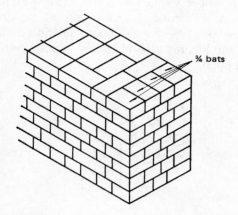

Figure 112   *Stopped end for a 2-brick wall in Dutch bond*

Self-assessment questions

1 The approximate angle of distribution of a load on a well-bonded wall should be
 (a) $67\frac{1}{2}$ degrees
 (b) 45 degrees
 (c) $22\frac{1}{2}$ degrees

2 A tie brick is one which is placed at the
 (a) internal angle of a quoin
 (b) in the interior of a thick wall
 (c) at the external angle of a wall

3 Garden-wall bonds are used primarily because they
 (a) are more economical
 (b) are quicker to build
 (c) provide a neat face on both sides of a 1-brick wall

4 Rat-trap bond is used
 (a) where high strength in the wall is required
 (b) because less bricks are used in the wall
 (c) to give a decorative finish to the walling

5 The bond shown in Figure 113 is called
 (a) Dutch bond
 (b) English garden-wall bond
 (c) Flemish garden-wall bond

Figure 113

6 Figure 114 shows the plan of a $1\frac{1}{2}$-brick junction wall in Flemish bond. Which is the correct bonding for the second course?
 (a)
 (b)
 (c)

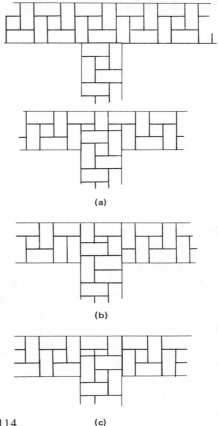

(a)

(b)

Figure 114   (c)

7 How does English garden-wall bond differ from Flemish garden-wall bond?

8 Draw an elevation of a piece of walling built in Dutch bond.

9 Draw the alternate plans of a 1-brick quoin built in Flemish bond.

10 Show alternative methods of forming a stopped end in a 2-brick wall built in English bond.

Chapter 5

Preparation for building

After reading this chapter you should be able to:

1 Have a good understanding of the various scales used for working drawings.
2 Set out right angles and simple walling using profiles.
3 Determine levels for walling from a datum peg.
4 Understand why the vegetable soil is removed from the area enclosed by the external walls of a building.
5 Have a good understanding of the methods of excavating for strip foundations and the safety precautions that should be taken.

Working drawings

When the drawings are received on the site they should be carefully studied so that the work to be done is fully understood. The groups of individual measurements should be collected and added up and checked against overall dimensions. Care should be taken before setting out any walling to ascertain from the drawing how the measurements are to be taken, for example:

Over all the walls (Figure 115(a))
Centre to centre (Figure 115(b))
In between the walls (Figure 115(c))

Drawings which show the work to be carried out are drawn to scale in one of the following general scales as used in the building industry:

1 : 5   that is $\frac{1}{5}$ full size
1 : 10   that is $\frac{1}{10}$ full size
1 : 20   that is $\frac{1}{20}$ full size
1 : 50   that is $\frac{1}{50}$ full size
1 : 100   that is $\frac{1}{100}$ full size
1 : 200   that is $\frac{1}{200}$ full size
1 : 500   that is $\frac{1}{500}$ full size

Whenever plans are produced it is logical that every effort be taken to ensure accuracy in the scaling of the drawings, but mistakes sometimes occur, and therefore figured dimensions should always be used in preference to scaled dimensions.

When any setting out has been done it should be carefully checked for accuracy by:

1 Re-checking overall measurements.
2 Measuring diagonals to ensure that sides are parallel and square to each other.
3 Taking measurements from fixed points other than the original ones from which the setting out was done.
4 Using the 3:4:5 rule for checking right angles – this is the method of measuring three sides of a triangle which has one angle of 90 degrees. The ratio of the measurements must always be in the proportion of 3:4:5, for example, 1.5 m:2 m:2.5 m or, 2.25 m:3 m: 3.75 m, and so on (Figures 116 and 117).

Setting out equipment

Measuring tapes

Before setting out any work the tape should be carefully checked for accuracy. Metallic linen tapes tend to stretch after they have been in use

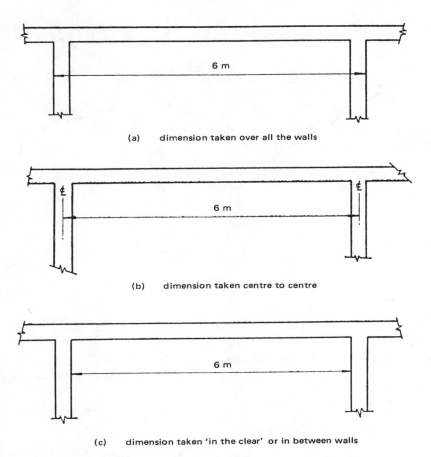

(a)   dimension taken over all the walls

(b)   dimension taken centre to centre

(c)   dimension taken 'in the clear' or in between walls

Figure 115   *Plans showing various ways in which measurements may be taken when setting out walls*

for some time, so it is wise to check them against a known or fixed length such as a steel tape or steel measuring chain. The steel chain or tape should be pulled taut and the metallic tape stretched alongside and their lengths compared.

Having checked the tape, mark the measurements on profiles, ensuring that each measurement is taken from the extended ring at the end of the tape (Figure 118).

Profiles

When setting out a building it is an advantage if the lines can be secured so that they are well clear of the building line. The trenches can then be dug without interfering with the lines.

Timber profiles may be erected for this. These

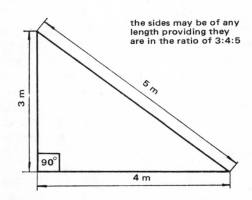

the sides may be of any length providing they are in the ratio of 3:4:5

Figure 116   *Setting out a right-angled triangle with the 3:4:5 rule*

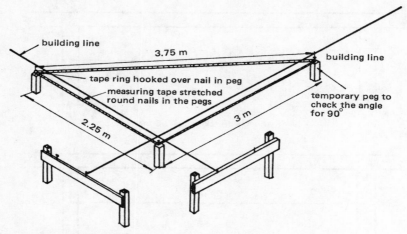

Figure 117   *The practical application of the 3:4:5 rule*

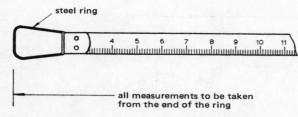

Figure 118   *Detail of the end of a measuring tape*

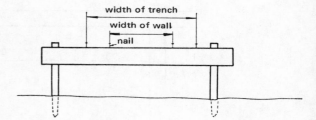

Figure 119   *A typical timber profile showing widths of wall and trench*

consist of pegs driven into the ground and boards nailed across them. The lines can then be stretched above the ground level well clear of any obstruction and may easily be checked for accuracy (Figures 119 and 120).

The width of the wall and the width of the foundation trench should be clearly marked on the profile with either nails, or saw cuts in the top of the profile. In both cases the full width of the wall and trench should be shown, otherwise if only one nail is driven in there is a possibility of the trench being dug on the wrong side of the line. Figure 121 shows a typical layout of profiles for a small building.

Datum level
When the lines are set out and checked for accuracy, the next step is to determine a basic level

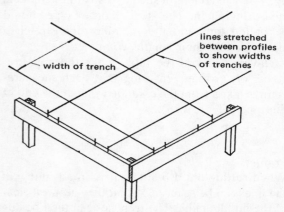

Figure 120   *An alternative method of erecting a profile at the corner of a building*

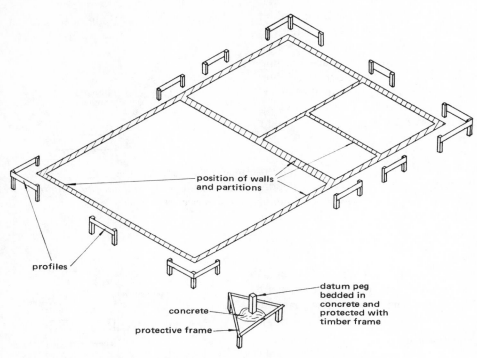

Figure 121   *A method of placing profiles in relation to the walls of a small building*

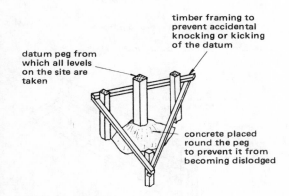

Figure 122   *Detail of a datum peg*

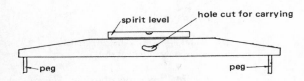

Figure 123   *A method of transferring a level from one peg to another*

from which all the measurements for the building to be erected on the site can be taken. This basic level is called the *datum level* (Figure 122). A peg is driven down until the top reaches the desired height and all the other levels are transferred from it. One method of transferring these levels is by using a *long levelling board* and spirit level. Before you use the board, check it for accuracy by placing it across two pegs and levelling with an accurate spirit level (see Chapter 3). Then reverse the levelling board but keep the spirit level in the same direction. If any adjustment is necessary plane off the upper edge of the levelling board (this being the shorter edge of the board) until it shows level in both directions (Figure 123).

Site work

Clearing vegetable soil
Before any building is constructed, the topsoil (or vegetable soil) should be dug and removed and in

some cases it may be cleared off the site. On some sites it may be required to be used as a top-tilth in areas to be seeded or turfed for lawns when the building work has been completed, in which case the soil should be stacked in a heap in some corner of the site where it is well clear of building operations. The reason for removing the vegetable soil is to prevent any plant life from growing underneath the floors of the building which would cause dampness in a timber floor and prevent a free flow of air around the timbers.

Dampness combined with a lack of ventilation underneath a timber floor provides ideal conditions for the growth of dry rot, which is a fungus that grows on and penetrates into timber and causes rapid decay.

Strip foundations

This type of foundation is most suitable for small structures. The trenches are dug to a convenient depth for each wall. The depth is dependent upon:

The nature of the soil upon which the building is going to rest.

The presence of water in the subsoil.

The possible effects of the atmosphere on the soil, such as rain and frost.

When the bottom of the trench has been reached and the level checked from the datum peg, the bottom of the trench should be well rammed so that any loose earth will be compacted ready to receive the concrete.

Construction work should be started in the trenches as soon as is reasonably possible after excavation is completed, because there is always a possibility of the sides of the trenches collapsing due to the effect of the weather.

In all cases trenches should be safeguarded as far as possible against collapse by:

1 Battering the sides of the trenches (Figure 124); or
2 Placing timbers in position against the sides of the trenches (Figure 125).

All work in trenches must be done with care and due regard to the safety of the people working in them. Risks must never be taken as they

can lead to accidents which may cause serious injuries to people working in the trench.

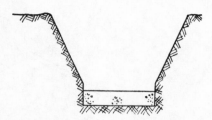

Figure 124   *Battering the sides of a trench*
This method needs no timber but requires more excavation and backfilling

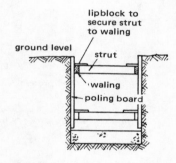

(a)   timbering the sides of a trench

this method involves the cost of timbering

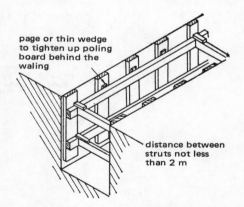

(b)   simple timbering for a shallow trench in a moderately compact soil

Figure 125   *Positioning timbers against the sides of the trenches*

Self-assessment questions

1   If a working detail is required it would normally be drawn to a scale of
    (a)   1:50
    (b)   1:20
    (c)   1:5

2   When checking the setting out of a right angle, two sides of which are 2.25 m and 3.0 m, the length of the third and longest side is
    (a)   3.25 m
    (b)   3.50 m
    (c)   3.75 m

3   A profile when applied to setting out is
    (a)   a point from which levels are taken
    (b)   a framework for fixing lines to
    (c)   a piece of hardboard cut to show the shape of a wall curved on plan

4   A datum level is
    (a)   the ground level
    (b)   a point from which all other levels are taken
    (c)   the foundation level

5   In trench timbering, a waling is the
    (a)   horizontal member holding the vertical members against the soil
    (b)   the vertical members of the timbering system
    (c)   the horizontal members across the trench

6   A timbering system is kept secure by
    (a)   nailing the members together
    (b)   screwing them together
    (c)   using wedges

7   Why are profiles used for setting out walling?

8   What is meant by 'strip foundations'?

9   Why is vegetable soil removed from the area enclosed by the external walls of a building?

10 State two ways in which the setting out of a building may be checked.

Chapter 6

Foundations, damp-proofing and ventilation

After reading this chapter you should be able to:

1 Have a sound understanding of how the weight of a building is transferred to the ground.

2 Have a knowledge of the minimum requirements for concrete mixes for foundations.

3 Be able to set out and lay simple foundations.

4 Be able to set out the footings and walling at the base of a structure.

5 Realize the importance of placing oversite concrete in a building.

6 Appreciate the reasons for preventing the passage of dampness from the ground to the inner surface of the wall.

7 Have a good knowledge of the various types of damp-proof courses in general use and their characteristics.

8 Have a good understanding of the construction of hollow timber floors and the necessity for providing adequate ventilation and damp-proofing.

Foundation concrete

Foundation concrete is placed at the base of walls to distribute the weight of the building as evenly as possible over a large area of the ground. To lay this concrete, first drive pegs into the bottom of the trench to indicate the required thickness of the concrete. This thickness will depend upon the load it has to carry, but in no case shall it be less than 150 mm, or equal to the length of the edge projecting from the face of the wall, whichever is the greater (Figure 126).

When the pegs have been checked for accuracy, place the concrete into the trench and smooth off with a shovel to the level of the pegs.

The width of the foundation is governed by the nature of the soil upon which the foundation is placed and the load it has to carry. The load is

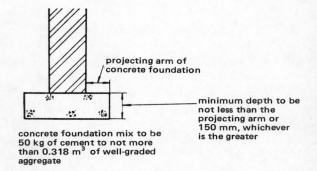

projecting arm of concrete foundation

minimum depth to be not less than the projecting arm or 150 mm, whichever is the greater

concrete foundation mix to be 50 kg of cement to not more than 0.318 m^3 of well-graded aggregate

Figure 126 *A concrete foundation*

usually given in kN/m per lineal metre of walling. The bearing pressure of the soil is the amount of weight that the soil can carry without any appreciable settlement and is usually given in N/m^2.

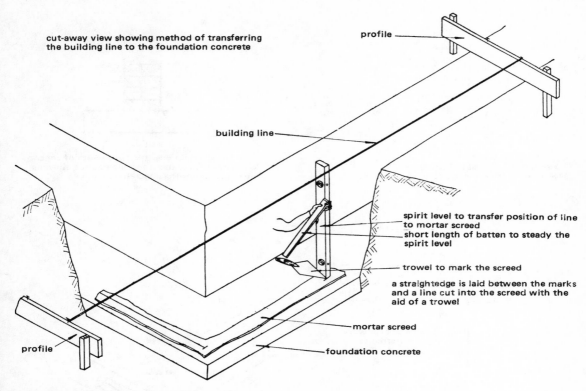

cut-away view showing method of transferring
the building line to the foundation concrete

profile

building line

spirit level to transfer position of line
to mortar screed
short length of batten to steady the
spirit level

trowel to mark the screed

a straightedge is laid between the marks
and a line cut into the screed with the
aid of a trowel

mortar screed

foundation concrete

profile

Figure 127   *Setting out the base of the wall*

The mix of the concrete should be in accordance with the strength desired. The Building Regulations state that the concrete should be composed of cement and fine and coarse aggregate conforming to BS 882 in the proportion of 50 kg of cement to not more than 0.1 m^3 of fine aggregate and 0.2 m^3 of coarse aggregate.

If the ground in which the foundation is being laid contains certain salts called sulphates, and many clays come within this category, take precautions to prevent deterioration of the concrete by the action of the sulphate. Among the most common of these salts are sodium sulphate (Glauber salts) and magnesium sulphate (Epsom salts), both of which have a harmful effect on ordinary Portland cement. In sulphate-bearing soils you are well-advised to use a sulphate-resisting cement for the concrete, which resists the action of the sulphates, and will provide a concrete that will last for a very long time.

After the concrete is laid, allow it to harden sufficiently for the brickwork to be set out and built on the top. In the case of concrete made with ordinary Portland cement, seven days should elapse before any brickwork is begun.

Setting out the base of the wall
A thin mortar screed is spread on the top of the concrete and the line of the wall is then transferred from the building lines stretched between the profiles by means of a spirit level or plumb rule which may be steadied with a batten (Figure 127).

Footings
In some cases the base of the wall may be spread out to distribute the weight of the wall over a greater area of concrete foundation and prevent the possibility of failure in the foundation by cracking. The courses which are used for this purpose are called footing courses (Figure 128).

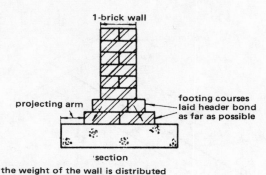

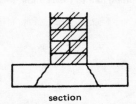

(a)   the weight of the wall is distributed over a greater area of concrete

(b)   a similar wall built over the same width of concrete foundation but without footing courses, showing the tendency for the concrete to crack

Figure 128   *Concrete foundations*

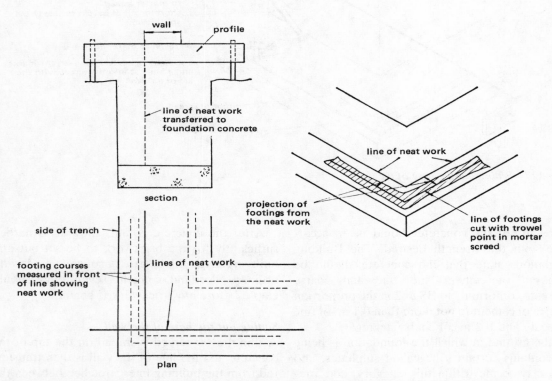

Figure 129   *An isometric view showing the method of setting out the footing courses for a quoin*

When you are setting out the wall, the main face should be marked out in the screed and the projection of the footing courses measured in front of the line (Figure 129).

The corners are then raised and the walling in between them built to a line which is stretched from each corner on each course.

The footing courses should be built in header bond as far as possible as this bond distributes more efficiently the load to be carried *across* the wall (Figure 128). No closers are used at the corners; Figures 130 and 131 show two methods that may be adopted to bond footing courses at an angle. In theory the quoin with the three-quarter

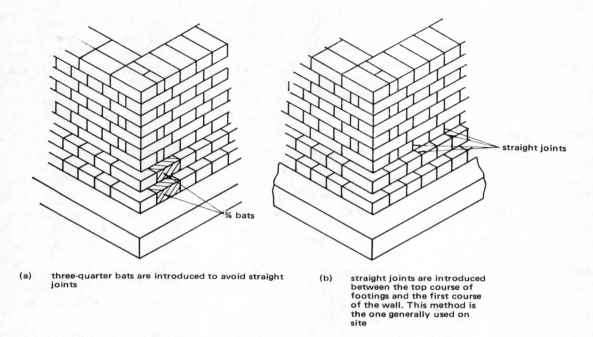

(a) three-quarter bats are introduced to avoid straight joints

(b) straight joints are introduced between the top course of footings and the first course of the wall. This method is the one generally used on site

Figure 130 *Bonding footing courses*

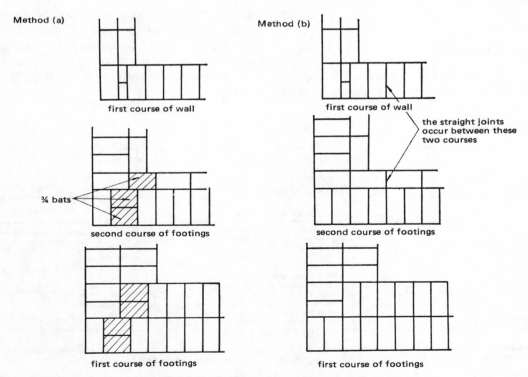

Figure 131 *Plans showing alternative methods of bonding footing courses*

bat (as shown in Method (a)) is the stronger because there are no straight joints in the wall, but in actual practice Method (b) is generally used as the straight joints do not create any major weakness, and in any case the lap could soon be gained by adjusting the mortar cross-joints.

Oversite concrete

This is a bed of concrete which is laid over the whole of the area within the external walls and is often called the *site concrete*. This must be provided to prevent rising damp from the ground entering the building and also to exclude the growth of plant life underneath the floor.

The Building Regulations require that the ground surface enclosed within the external walls shall be covered with a layer of concrete not less than 100 mm thick composed of cement and fine and coarse aggregate conforming to BS 882, in the proportion of 50 kg of cement to not more than 0.1 m^3 of fine aggregate and 0.2 m^3 of coarse aggregate, properly laid on a bed of hardcore, clean clinker, broken brick or similar material and finished with a trowel or spade (Figure 132).

Damp-proof courses

The Building Regulations require that no wall or pier shall permit the passage of moisture from the ground to the inner surface or to any part of the building that would be harmfully affected by such moisture. Therefore, a damp-proof course must be provided at a height of not less than 150 mm above the ground level adjoining the wall. The types of materials that would be very suitable for damp-proof courses would include the following:

Reinforced plastic sheeting.

A layer of bituminous felt.

Bituminous felt with a very thin layer of lead in the middle.

Two or more courses of engineering bricks laid in English bond in Portland cement mortar 1:3.

Two courses of slate laid half-bond in Portland cement mortar 1:3.

Asphalt in one or two layers laid hot across the wall.

A layer of non-ferrous metal such as sheet lead, copper or zinc.

A layer of waterproofed cement mortar.

All walls, including sleeper walls, shall be provided with a d.p.c. to safeguard them and the floors from becoming wet through rising damp. In timber floors the damp-proof course must be laid immediately below the lowest timber member, but in solid floors the d.p.c. is laid at the same level as the upper surface of the floor (Figure 132).

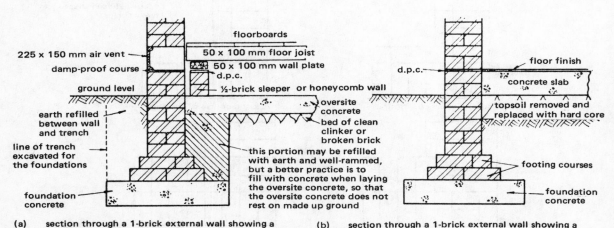

(a) section through a 1-brick external wall showing a hollow floor construction

(b) section through a 1-brick external wall showing a solid floor construction

Figure 132   *1-brick external walls showing hollow and solid floor construction*

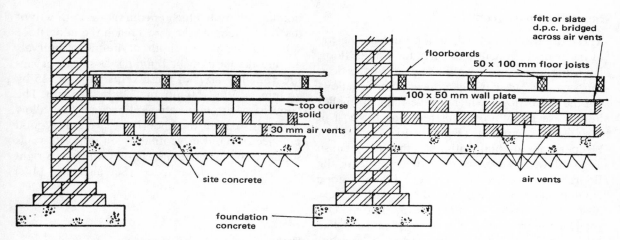

Figure 133   *Alternative methods of building 112 mm honeycomb or sleeper walls*

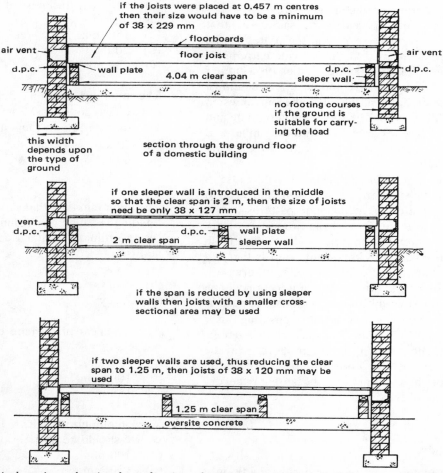

Figure 134   *Typical sections showing how the size of joists for a domestic building may be reduced by the introduction of sleeper walls*

Sleeper or honeycomb walls

These are dwarf walls which are built on the top of the oversite concrete to carry the timber floor. By using these dwarf walls the span of the floor joists can be considerably reduced, thereby allowing the use of joists which are very much smaller in cross-sectional area, thus reducing the cost of the timber required (Figures 133 and 134). Sleeper walls are built with holes through them so as to allow a free passage of air underneath the floor. Thus, if the timbers are kept dry and a good circulation of air is maintained there will be very little chance of dry rot attacking the timbers. Dry rot is a fungus, which is a living plant, and like other plants, in order to live, it must have moisture to provide food, oxygen and a suitable temperature to germinate the spores.

Fungi produce spores in the same way that other plants produce seeds and the spores can be carried in the air by draughts or wind currents. If one or more of these spores settles on a timber member which is moist and in a warm atmosphere, the timber is very likely to become infested by the dry rot spore. The spore will germinate and thrust long threads or hyphae into the timber and begin to feed on it, causing the cells of the timber to break down.

Dry rot (*Merulius lacrymans*) will cause a timber to become friable and soft and also to crack in squares or rectangular patterns across and with the grain. One of the properties of dry rot is its power to penetrate walls to find fresh timber to infest. The important point is that dry rot must have a source of moisture, otherwise it will die. In view of this the risk of infection will be reduced considerably if the underfloor space is kept dry; one of the best means of ensuring this is to have good currents of air circulating underneath the floor when, although spores may be blown beneath the floor, there will be little chance of their germinating because of the dry condition which exists.

Ventilation

If air circulates quite freely underneath a floor, it will absorb any free moisture, thus preventing the humid condition which encourages the growth of dry rot. To enable the air to reach the underfloor space, air vents are built at frequent intervals around the base of the building, as shown in Figure 132. The sizes of these vents may be 225 by 75 mm, 225 by 150 mm or, 225 by 225 mm. The larger sizes are more efficient because they allow more air to enter the underfloor space. It is good practice to build in ventilators on opposite walls so that draughts of air are created which pass right across the underfloor space. (See also page 114.)

Self-assessment questions

1 The minimum thickness of foundation concrete is
   (a)   150 mm
   (b)   200 mm
   (c)   250 mm

2 The minimum amount of cement to 0.1 m^3 of fine aggregate and 0.2 m^3 of coarse aggregate for concrete in foundations is
   (a)   70 kg
   (b)   60 kg
   (c)   50 kg

3 The minimum time that should elapse before building walling on foundation concrete (using ordinary Portland cement) after it is laid is
   (a)   3 days
   (b)   5 days
   (c)   7 days

4 The thickness of oversite concrete shall be not less than
   (a)   75 mm
   (b)   100 mm
   (c)   150 mm

5 The minimum height that a damp-proof course should be above ground level is
   (a)   100 mm
   (b)   150 mm
   (c)   200 mm

6 The bond generally used in footing course so far as is possible is
   (a) English bond
   (b) Flemish bond
   (c) Header bond

7 Sleeper walls are built with spaces between the bricks because
   (a) they are quicker to build
   (b) they allow air to circulate under the floor
   (c) they need less bricks to build them

8 Why is foundation concrete placed at the base of a wall?

9 What factors govern the width of foundations?

10 What are the conditions which are most likely to help the growth of dry rot in buildings and how are these conditions overcome, so far as is possible, in a structure?

Chapter 7

Methods of work

After reading this chapter you should be able to:

1 Know what the first essentials are in building.

2 Know how to keep brickwork horizontal and vertical.

3 Understand the need for gauging brickwork and the methods that are used to keep brickwork to correct gauge.

4 Understand the general procedures for building walling including the use of corner profiles and tingles.

5 Set out piers and openings in walling including the introduction of broken bonds.

6 Appreciate the importance of protecting face work during the erection of the structure and the methods that may be used to provide such protection.

7 Allow provision for additional walling and partitions, also for pipes and other services.

To sell an article you must make it attractive to the customer. In production engineering, firms go to great lengths to ensure that their products have a finish that is both durable and attractive to the eye.

The same thing *must* apply in the building industry, and a bricklayer should realize that his work is the outside of the article, and therefore should be well-made and look pleasing to the customer. Brickwork which has been done by good craftsmen using first-class bricks has a very attractive appearance which will last for a long time. On the other hand, if the work has been carried out in a slipshod manner it will be a thoroughly bad advertisement both for the craftsman and the builder by whom he is employed, and this may well prove to have an adverse effect on the business on which both rely.

The first essentials in building are that the work should:

Be vertical
Be truly horizontal

Have perpends in line and truly vertical
Have a true surface along its face

Plumbing

For a wall to be vertical it is vital to ensure that the corners or quoins are truly perpendicular or *plumb*. As each quoin brick is laid it should be plumbed with the aid of a plumb rule and plumb-bob, or more usually in these days, with a bricklayer's spirit level (Figure 135). If a corner leans out, it is said to *overhang*; if it leans back, it is said to *batter*. Some craftsmen assert that it is better to build a corner with a very slight batter, but in actual practice it is far more satisfactory to keep the work truly plumb.

In first-class face work the perpends should be kept vertical, and this is achieved by plumbing the perpends with the aid of a spirit level, and putting a small pencil mark where the bricks are to be laid (Figure 143). Do not use indelible pencils for this purpose since they cause serious staining.

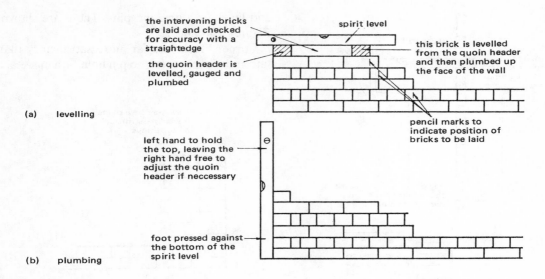

the intervening bricks are laid and checked for accuracy with a straightedge

the quoin header is levelled, gauged and plumbed

spirit level

this brick is levelled from the quoin header and then plumbed up the face of the wall

pencil marks to indicate position of bricks to be laid

(a) levelling

left hand to hold the top, leaving the right hand free to adjust the quoin header if neccessary

foot pressed against the bottom of the spirit level

(b) plumbing

Figure 135 *Method of plumbing and levelling a corner*

Levelling

If a wall is out of level it is commonly said to *have a pig in it* and a wall like this is rather unsightly. Even if a wall has been built out of level for part of the height and then corrected by either grinding down the end which is high, that is, using very thin bed joints, or bringing up the end which is low, it will stand out as amateurish and give the work a poor appearance. It is, therefore, necessary to keep a constant check on the work throughout its construction.

The method that is usually adopted is to fix a *peg* at each corner of the building. These are short lengths of wood about 50 by 25 by 250 mm (Figure 136). The tops of these pegs are carefully levelled with each other from the permanent datum peg described in Chapter 5, before the brickwork is begun. On small buildings this may be done with the aid of a long levelling board and spirit level in a way similar to that also described in Chapter 5.

Gauging

A gauge rod of 37 by 37 mm timber and of a convenient length must then be set out to show the height of the brick courses. These courses should be made to suit the thickness of the bricks plus the required thickness of joint. This is called keeping the work to gauge, and is commonly four courses to 305 mm. Alternatively it may be four courses to 325 mm or five courses to 325 mm, according to the size of bricks used. If the job is only a small one, then the courses may be pencilled on the gauge rods. If, however, the building is a large one and the gauge rods are to be in use for quite a long time, then it is a better practice to make small saw cuts at the course marks. For convenience the gauge can be used as a *storey rod*, and the length of the rod is usually at least the height of a storey so that the datum pegs can be fixed at each floor level.

In addition to the courses, various other heights can be marked on one of the plain faces of the rod, such as heights of sills, arches, air bricks, plinths and string courses. These marks on the gauge rod serve as a reminder to the craftsman during building operations so that no special feature is forgotten. This will obviate the necessity for pulling down and rebuilding which is expensive and most uneconomical.

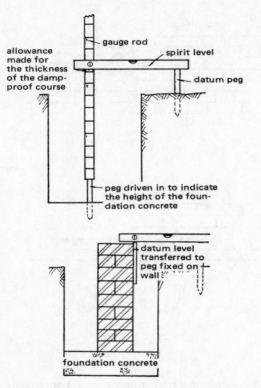

Figure 136 *Sections showing the applications of a datum peg*

Erecting a corner

When the pegs are fixed and the gauge rod set out, the corners should be erected. The corners should not be too large since it is much more economical to run a wall with the aid of a line than to build up large portions of walling in the form of corners. The corners should preferably be raked back, as shown in Figure 137, since toothing is frowned upon by many clerks of works, because of the difficulty of ensuring a solid joint when the bricks are placed, when building up to the toothings. In such work a line of weakness could occur, and if there were any slight movement in the foundation, the defect would be quite likely to show and cause cracking.

Working along the line

When the corners are built, the walling in between can be worked with the aid of either corner blocks

and lines, or a line and pins. These are shown in Figures 138 and 139.

Corner blocks are far more satisfactory than a line and pins, because no pin holes are made in the

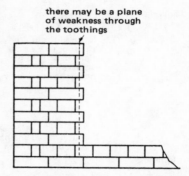

(a)   this method of building a corner should be avoided if possible

(b)   this method should be used if a large corner is required to be erected

Figure 137   *Alternative methods of corner construction*

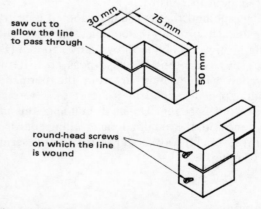

Figure 138   *Detail of a typical corner block*

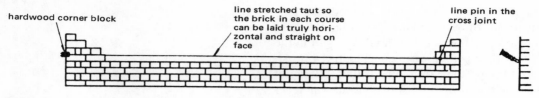

Figure 139 *Alternative methods of supporting a line at 'the end' of a wall*

wall, and the pins do not get bent by being hammered into hard mortar. Once the line has been set to the length of the wall, no further adjustment is necessary, since it is simply a case of sliding the corner block up the wall to the height of each course.

Corner profiles

Instead of building corners first, an alternative method can be used in many cases, particularly with boundary walls or long walls having a plain façade. This is to erect corner profiles. These are of planed timber fixed vertically and braced to prevent their moving, so that the line can be secured, as in Figure 140, without any necessity for corners. With this method the gauge can be marked on the profile and the expense of building the corner is considerably reduced. Care must be

exercised to ensure that the profile is straight and fixed rigidly in an upright position.

There are also patent corner profiles on the market which serve the same purpose in a very effective way.

If the wall is a long one then the line will tend to sag in the middle. To offset this, *tingles* should be provided – one or more (Figure 141). The height of these can be checked:

1 With the gauge rod from a datum peg fixed at that point; or
2 By the corner-man *sighting through the line*; any discrepancy can easily be seen and corrected.

Broken bonds

Now the face bond should be set out. The window

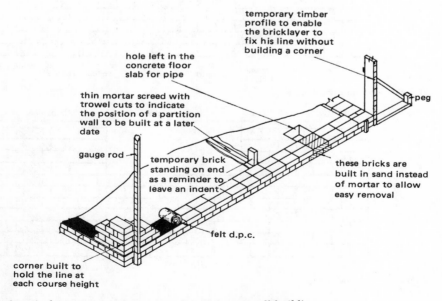

Figure 140 *A typical setting out of an external wall for a small building*

and door openings are clearly marked, the perpends to suit those openings set out, and if there are any broken bonds these should be built in the middle of the openings or piers (Figure 142). An important point to bear in mind is that setting out of the face bond will differ on adjacent wall faces (Figure 143).

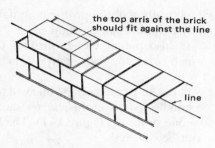

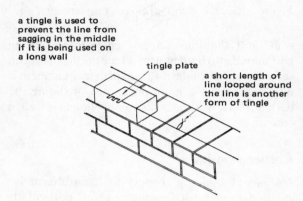

Figure 141 *The use of a tingle*

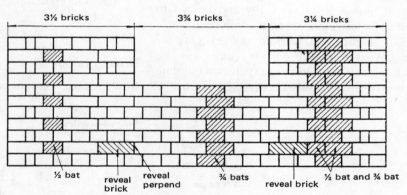

(a)   three broken bonds in English bond

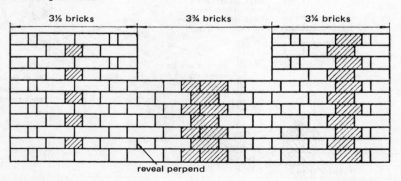

(b)   broken bonds in Flemish bond

Figure 142 *Broken bonds in English and Flemish bond*

Figure 143   *An isometric view showing the setting out of face bonds on adjoining faces*

It is far better if broken bonds can be avoided altogether, but where openings and piers do not allow for brick sizes, the broken bonds should be carefully set out. Once their position has been settled, this should be maintained throughout the height of the wall. *On no account should a closer be built in the middle of the wall; it should only be placed next to the quoin header.* If a wall is longer

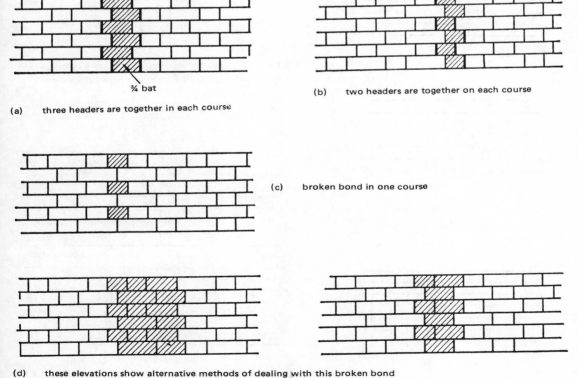

Figure 144   *Typical broken bonds in Flemish bond*

than brick size by 56 mm, then do not place a closer in the middle of the wall, but a half bat and three-quarter bat instead.

Examples of broken bonds are shown in Figures 144–149. Figure 145 shows three examples of broken bonds in stretcher bond. Figure 146 illustrates three broken bonds which are commonly found in English bond and Figure 147 shows two broken bonds in Flemish garden-wall bond.

Figure 148 shows how broken bonds would be introduced in Dutch bond. Note how the patterns are formed by the cut bricks.

In every case, regardless of the bond, the pier starts at each end with identical bricks, that is, header or stretcher, and the broken bond is worked as near as possible to the centre of the pier.

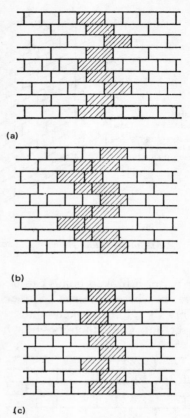

(a)

(b)

(c)

Figure 146   *Alternative ways of placing a three-quarter bat in a wall built with English garden-wall bond*

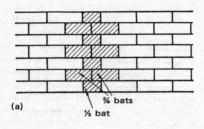

(a)   ¾ bats
        ½ bat

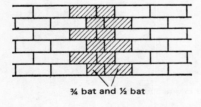

¾ bat and ½ bat

(b)

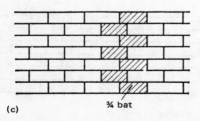

(c)   ¾ bat

Figure 145   *Typical broken bonds in stretcher bond*

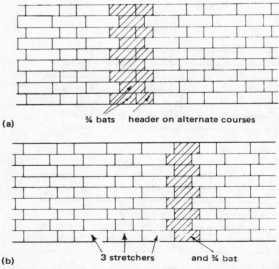

(a)   ¾ bats   header on alternate courses

(b)   3 stretchers   and ¾ bat

Figure 147   *Typical broken bonds in Flemish garden-wall bond*

completion of the walling, the small area of temporary brickwork removed to allow a large or small pipe to be inserted through the wall and become built-in), which may be needed by plumbers or other craftsmen, are clearly shown (Figure 140). Cutting away after the wall is built is a great waste of money. Close co-operation between crafts is essential and you would be wise to cultivate this habit right from the beginning of your career in the building industry.

Figure 148   *Typical broken bonds in Dutch bond*

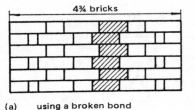

(a)   **using a broken bond**

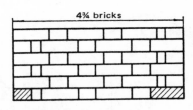

(b)   **using a reverse bond**
the reveals show reverse bond

Figure 149   *Two methods of bonding a pier in Flemish bond*

Reverse bond

There is an exception to this rule (page 79), called a reverse bond. In some cases a three-quarter bat may be avoided in the middle of the pier by using a stretcher at one end, and header closer at the other end. Figure 149 shows the same length pier built with a broken bond in the middle and an alternative method using reverse bond in Flemish bond. Figure 150 shows a similar comparison in English bond and Figure 151 in Dutch bond. Figure 152 illustrates the bonding of similar piers in stretcher bond.

In all examples it will be seen that the reverse bond is generally the neatest and the most economical method of bonding these piers, but remember that the reveal bricks will not correspond with each other.

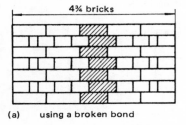

(a)   **using a broken bond**

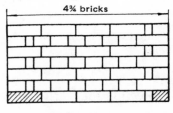

(b)   **using reverse bond**

Figure 150   *Two methods of bonding a pier in English bond*

Allowing for future work

When commencing a wall, take care that all partitions are set out correctly and clearly marked, and that the positions of air bricks and any sand courses (small areas of brickwork built in damp sand which allow the work to proceed, and, after

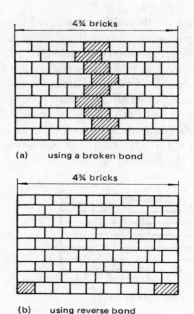

Figure 151 *Two methods of bonding a pier in Dutch bond*

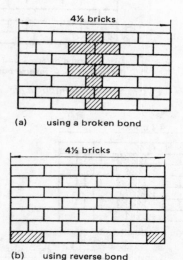

Figure 152 *Two methods of bonding a pier in stretcher bond*

Protecting the work against damage

Face work should be well-protected against damage while it is being built and also after it has been erected. It is expensive to clean down brickwork, or to cut out and replace damaged work, and therefore it should be kept as clean as possible during the building by:

1 Cutting the surplus mortar off cleanly with the trowel.
2 Leaving a small gap of about 100–125 mm between scaffold boards and wall to allow any droppings to pass through.
3 Turning back the scaffold board nearest the wall during wet weather and at the end of each day. This prevents the wall being splashed by rain rebounding from the scaffold, or running off the board nearest the wall and being blown on the face work.
4 If any concreting operations are being done nearby, covering the face work adequately. If any concrete falls on the face work, you must wash it off immediately, since at a later stage it would be very difficult to remove.
5 Protecting angles at entrances which are being used by wheelbarrows, oversailing courses or any projecting features which are liable to be damaged by falling bricks or tools, by fixing thin sawn timber securely over them. The timber is a little costly, but not nearly as costly as trying to repair brickwork damaged through lack of protection.
6 Using polythene sheeting; work which must be kept clean during operations (such as tumbling-in to buttresses, plinth courses and so on) can easily be protected thus.
7 After the joints have been raked out for pointing at a later date, brushing them well. If this is not done, the loose particles may be washed out of the joints by rain and cause staining.

As a general rule, where expensive face work is being used it is a sound policy to protect all angles and projections, and to keep the face clean. It is cheaper in the long run and indicates that the job is being efficiently managed.

Indents

When leaving indents for the bonding of partitions to a main wall, take care to ensure that the indent is left wide enough to accommodate the partition block. In general the indent should be

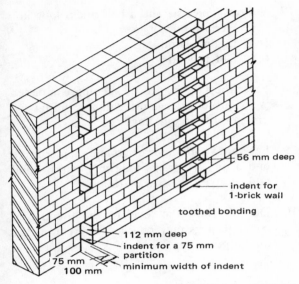

56 mm deep

indent for
1-brick wall

toothed bonding

112 mm deep
indent for a 75 mm
partition
minimum width of indent

75 mm
100 mm

the perpends should be
kept vertical right up
the face of the wall

Figure 153   *Block bonding*

from 25 to 37 mm wider than the thickness of the partition. Thus, if the partition is to be 50 mm wide, then the width of the indent should be 75–87 mm. If it is for a 100 mm partition, the indent should be 125–137 mm wide, and so on (Figure 153). You should try to visualize the building of the partition at a later date, and foresee the difficulty of putting a 100 mm wide block into an indent precisely 100 mm wide. Treat indents left for ½-brick or 1-brick walls similarly.

Clean out indents and toothings thoroughly before the wall is completed to avoid the wasteful necessity of cutting out hard mortar with a hammer and chisel when the partitions are being built. Keep the indents truly plumb. If this is not done you will need to cut away the sides of the indents with a hammer and chisel, thus causing unnecessary work and delay in building the partition.

Sand courses

It is always easier and more efficient to lay bricks in sand at the place where a pipe is to pass through a wall at a later date, than to hack out the bricks with a hammer and chisel, as was explained previously. The bricks which have been used in the sand courses can be used for filling in the hole afterwards, so there is no waste of bricks and little extra in labour cost, as there would be if the hole had to be cut out afterwards (Figure 140). You should remember particularly the indents or sand courses when you are working *along the line*, since it is not uncommon for a high proportion of the cutting away of brickwork on a site to be given to apprentices to do.

Incidently, when brickwork is required to be cut away to provide access for services, or for any reason, it is most important that the eyes are protected by wearing safety goggles as laid down in The Protection of Eyes Regulations.

Provision of a key for plaster

If the interior face of the external wall is to be plastered, then *fluted* or *keyed* bricks should be used. These provide an excellent means of keying the plaster to the wall face. If these bricks are not readily available, use plain, common bricks instead, then rake out the joints. This method is not as efficient as using keyed bricks.

Self-assessment questions

1   When building a corner it is best to erect it
    (a)   with a slight overhang
    (b)   upright
    (c)   with a slight batter

2   A gauge rod is used to
    (a)   check the distances between walling
    (b)   check that perpends are kept vertical
    (c)   check the heights of courses

3   Corner blocks are
    (a)   prepared pieces of wood to enable lines to be secured at corners
    (b)   profiles erected at corners to avoid building the corners before the general walling
    (c)   temporary piers built to fix lines to

4   A tingle is
    (a)   a piece of batten fixed to a wall from which levels are taken
    (b)   the means of correcting the sag in a line
    (c)   the means of fixing a line to a profile

5   Sand courses are
    (a)   those which allow easy removal of bricks from a wall
    (b)   decorative courses in brickwork
    (c)   courses laid with special facing bricks

6   Keyed bricks are those which are used for
    (a)   decorative courses in brickwork
    (b)   bonding in partitions at internal angles
    (c)   walls which are to be plastered

7   Set out a pier six and a half bricks long in
    (a)   Flemish bond
    (b)   English bond
    (c)   Dutch bond

8   State the importance of keeping completed work protected against damage during the erection of the building.

9   Set out two methods of bonding a pier three and a quarter bricks long in Flemish bond and compare the two methods.

10 Describe how the level of the foundation concrete pegs may be transferred from the datum peg.

Chapter 8

Blockwork

After reading this chapter you should be able to:

1 Have a sound knowledge of the erection of walls built in blockwork.
2 Have a knowledge of the manufacture of precast units.
3 Have an appreciation of the weight of precast units and their handling.
4 Know the various types of mortars which are suitable for blockwork.
5 Have a good knowledge of the various sizes of precast blocks in general use.
6 Understand the importance of setting out bonding for walling, and the avoidance of broken bonds, so far as is possible.
7 Have a good knowledge of the methods of working when building block walls.
8 Have a good knowledge of general bonding.
9 Appreciate the importance of buttressing walls and piers.
10 Understand what is meant by the term 'drying shrinkage', and how precautions may be taken to avoid damage, so far as is possible, through this movement.
11 Understand the construction of walling at openings and parapet walling.

Blocks

Walling built with precast blocks may be separated into two main categories:

1 load-bearing
2 non-load-bearing

In this chapter the emphasis will be on the first group as the non-load-bearing units are mainly used in conjunction with partitions, which are described in more detail in Chapter 14.

The units which are used for blockwork are precast in moulds and compacted with the aid of vibration, or moulding machines involving the use of compressed air, or a combination of both.

These blocks are usually made of concrete comprised of cement and aggregate. The cement is usually ordinary Portland or rapid hardening, although other types may be used for blocks which are intended for special purposes. (See also *Brickwork 2*, Chapter 16.) The aggregates may consist of crushed natural stone or rock, shingle or ballast. Admixtures may also be used to provide added workability during their manufacture.

Density of blocks

The resulting blocks will, of course, vary in weight according to the density of the aggregates used in their manufacture, but if they are made too large they may prove to be too heavy for one man to handle comfortably. Therefore, if large units are required then it will be necessary for them to be made hollow. If the hollow block is to be regarded as equivalent to a solid unit then the Building Regulations state that it must have an aggregate volume of not less than 50 per cent of the total volume of the block calculated from its overall dimensions. It must also have a resistance to crushing (expressed in newtons per square millimetre of gross horizontal area) of not less than 2.8 N/mm^2, if the blocks are to be used for the construction of a wall of a residential building having one or two-storeys, and the height of each storey does not exceed 2.7 m. In all other circumstances the blocks shall have a resistance to crushing of not less than 7 N/mm^2.

Mortar for blockwork

The mortar for such blockwork may be composed of Portland cement (either ordinary or rapid hardening), lime (either non-hydraulic or semi-hydraulic) and fine aggregate in the proportion (measured by volume of the materials when dry) of one part cement, one part lime and not more than six parts of fine aggregate.

Alternatively if a dense mortar is required for special purposes then a mortar composed of one part of cement (ordinary Portland cement or rapid hardening cement) to four parts of fine aggregate may be used.

Block sizes

British Standard 2028 defines a block as a walling unit exceeding the length, width or height as specified for bricks in British Standard 3921. The height of the block must not exceed either its length or six times its thickness.

The density of a block may be calculated by dividing the mass of the block by the overall volume including holes and cavities.

Precast concrete blocks are specified as Type A, that is, those having a block density of not less than 1500 kg/m^3, and Type B having a density of less than 1500 kg/m^3. Their sizes are listed in Table 6.

Table 6 *Block sizes*

Type of block	Length × height (co-ordinating size) (mm)	Thickness (work size) (mm)
A	400 × 100	75, 90, 100, 140, 190
	400 × 200	140, 190
	450 × 225	75, 90, 100, 140, 190, 225
B	400 × 100 ⎫ 400 × 200 ⎭	75, 90, 140, 190
	450 × 200 ⎫ 450 × 225 ⎪ 450 × 300 ⎬ 600 × 200 ⎪ 600 × 225 ⎭	75, 90, 100, 140, 215

An allowance of 10 mm is included in all the co-ordinating sizes for the vertical and horizontal joints; thus the 'work size' of a 400 by 100 mm block would be 390 by 90 mm, and so on.

The laying of blocks

The use of blocks has increased over the years because of the economics of handling and purchasing over normal brickwork; the theory being that one block takes the place of a number of brick units, but in fact the weight and the bulk of the blocks usually means that more time is taken to lay each unit. It is also extremely difficult to obtain a fair-faced wall when laying blocks and requires a great deal of skill and care if a pleasing fair-face is to be produced. This is mainly due to the fact that the blocks will vary somewhat in depth and consequently there is only a slim chance to manoeuvre with the adjustment of the bed joints, and once a block is laid there is only a small inclination to lift it off the mortar to re-lay it, owing to the weight of the block and difficulty in handling. Also, when laying the corner blocks, special care must be taken to ensure that the quoin block is not slightly dislodged when the block is laid adjacent to it.

Problems may also arise in the bonding of piers and walling, particularly where broken bonds have to be introduced, as many types of blocks are very difficult to cut leaving them with a neat edge to the cut. So it is good practice, before commencing the actual laying of the blocks, to set out the bonding with 'dry' blocks, that is, using no mortar but making allowances for the vertical joints. This will ensure that the wall is constructed with a minimum of broken bonds in the fair-faced work.

There are, however, companies who will supply special units in addition to the normal size of blocks, such as three-quarter, half and quarter lengths; also corner blocks, which are full-length on one face and half-length on the other, thus allowing the wall to be built from the quoin in half-bond without having to introduce a cut block (Figure 154).

In general, the rules for laying blocks are similar to those for the laying of bricks, that is, in foundations the block walls are built off the foundation concrete in the same manner as for brickwork, and allowance must be made for underfloor ventilation if the ground floor is of hollow timber construction. Also, a damp prevention must be laid in the wall at a height of not less than 150 mm above the adjacent ground level.

Datum pegs should be fixed at all points where the wall changes direction, such as quoins and internal angles, then the courses may be 'gauged' from these datums to ensure that the work is kept level all round the structure.

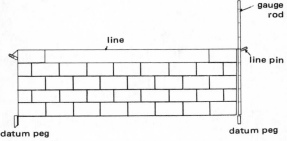

Figure 155   *Method of building with blockwork*

The quoin and internal angle blocks are then laid, plumbed and levelled, then a line is stretched tautly between these blocks, and the intervening blocks are laid to the line (Figure 155).

As the work becomes higher, the weight of the blocks can make it difficult for the craftsman to manoeuvre them around the line and it is at this stage that special care must be taken to ensure that blocks are 'laid to the line'. The craftsman must resist the temptation to leave any badly laid block because of the effort required to remove it and re-lay it.

Bonding

The bonding of quoins are shown in Figures 156, 157 and 158, using various sizes of blocks.

In general, a wall having a thickness of 190 mm and not exceeding 3.5 metres in height, then it should not exceed 12 metres in length. If it should exceed 3.5 metres in height then its length must not exceed 9 metres. Because of this it is necessary for a long wall to be supported by buttressing walls or piers, and Figures 159 and 160 show methods of bonding such walls and piers.

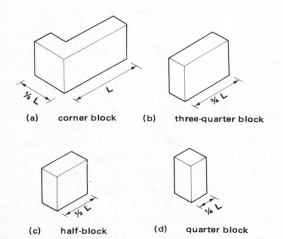

(a)   corner block   (b)   three-quarter block

(c)   half-block   (d)   quarter block

Figure 154   *Special blocks*

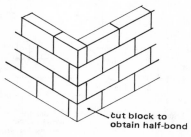

Figure 156   *Method of building a quoin with 100 mm blocks*

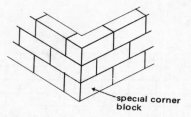

Figure 157   *Building a quoin using special corner units*

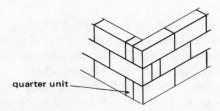

Figure 158   *Building a quoin using quarter units*

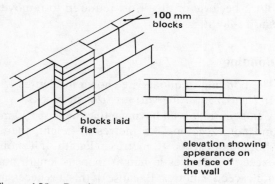

Figure 159   *Bonding an attached pier into a main wall*

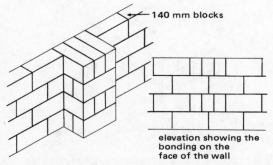

Figure 160   *Bonding a buttressing pier into a main wall*

Junction walls

It is often inconvenient to build the junction wall at the same time as the main wall and in such cases provision must be made for the junction wall to be bonded into the main wall by leaving indents, as shown in Figure 161. These indents should be carefully plumbed with each other and an allowance of 20 mm over the width of the partition made to permit easy entry of the blocks into the indents.

When setting out the bonding for a partition wall it is difficult to avoid the cutting of blocks, and, as previously stated, this can be difficult and uneconomic. In certain cases it may be permissible to build in reinforcing mesh in the main walling to tie in the partition wall. This will avoid excessive cutting at the internal angle. However, it is most important to remember that this reinforcement must be kept plumb and well-anchored into the main walling (Figure 162).

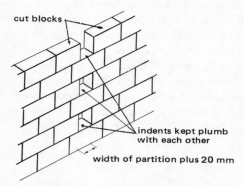

Figure 161   *Method of providing bonding for a partition*

Drying shrinkage

Precast units inevitably will have considerable movement due to the shrinking of the blocks when they dry out. Similarly, if they become wet there will be some expansion, therefore, it is necessary in long walls to introduce continuous vertical joints, commonly referred to as 'construction joints' though they are primarily intended to control any cracking which may occur due to the movement in the wall. These joints may be filled with a mastic compound or covered with a metal cover plate.

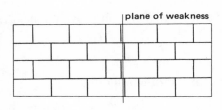

Figure 163 *A broken bond which has been badly set out which can often be avoided by setting out the bond 'dry' first*

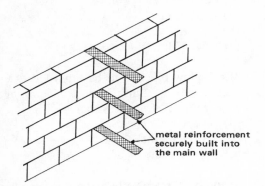

Figure 162 *An alternative method of tying-in a partition*

Broken bonds

When bonding fair-faced piers and walling it is difficult to avoid the introduction of broken bonds as so often the distance between openings and also between buttressing walls and piers does not allow for actual unit size. In block work this is particularly difficult as larger units allow little room for adjustment in the vertical joints. When broken bonds are unavoidable it is important not to put in cut blocks which only allow a small amount of lap (see Figure 163), as this can create a weak plane in the wall and any movement due to drying shrinkage, etc., may result in cracking down the line of joints. Figures 164 and 165 show how to avoid broken bonds of less than half-block size. It is also good practice to use the purpose-made units, that is, three-quarter, half and quarter lengths so far as is possible in order to avoid cutting the blocks by hand. But where such cutting is unavoidable they should be carefully marked and then cut with a club hammer and narrow bolster, pitching tool, or cold chisel, depending upon quality and size of the block to be cut. If a mechanical saw is available then blocks which are to be cut for fair-faced work may be first cut with a groove about 8 mm deep on the face of the block and then the block finished off

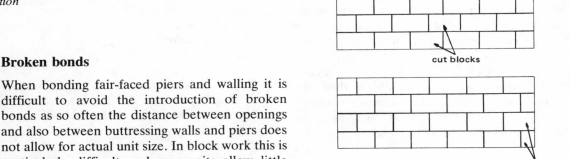

Figure 164 *Alternative arrangements showing how to avoid broken bonds of less than half-block size*

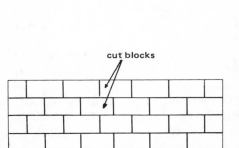

Figure 165 *Where the broken bond is greater than a half-block then the bonding is straightforward*

with hand tools. This will provide a neat edge to the cut block.

Door and window openings

Openings may be bridged with precast or cast *in situ* lintels. These are described in more detail in Chapter 9. The texture on face should match the surrounding block work, and the height of the lintel should be in line with the courses in the main walling, otherwise this will involve unnecessary cutting over the lintel.

Similarly, the sills for window openings should match the surrounding work (details of suitable sills will be found in Chapter 9).

When using blocks for cavity walling difficulty may be encountered when sealing the cavity at window or door openings because of the smallness of the cut, and great care must be exercised when building the reveals. However, some suppliers will provide specially cast blocks which have returns on them to suit the size of cavity. These of course are more expensive than the ordinary block but generally are more economical because of the amount of time that may be spent in cutting blocks to seal the cavity.

Parapet walls

The Building Regulations state that the thickness of a parapet wall be not less than one-quarter of its height and (a) if the wall is of solid construction the thickness shall be the same as the wall on which it is carried, or 190 mm, whichever is less; or (b) if the parapet is of cavity construction then it shall be the same thickness as the wall on which it is carried.

The capping of the parapet wall should be in units to match the general walling in texture and in size.

As an alternative to using precast units, the capping may be made with plastic units. The Ful-bora PVC coping is a system which is eminently suitable for this type of work, and provides an excellent finish to fair-faced walling in brickwork and blockwork.

Self-assessment questions

1   Assuming the density of concrete to be 2400 kg/m^3, the weight of a precast block 450 by 225 by 90 mm is
(a)   15.22 kg
(b)   18.46 kg
(c)   21.87 kg

2   If a hollow block is to be regarded as equivalent to a solid unit it must have an aggregate volume of not less than
(a)   40 per cent
(b)   50 per cent
(c)   60 per cent

3   If the blocks are to be used for a small residential building they shall have a resistance to crushing of not less than
(a)   2.8 N/mm^2
(b)   3.8 N/mm^2
(c)   4.8 N/mm^2

4   If the blocks are to be used on a building having three-storeys their resistance to crushing must not be less than
(a)   5 N/mm^2
(b)   6 N/mm^2
(c)   7 N/mm^2

5   If a cement/lime/sand mix is to be used for the mortar for blockwork, the maximum volume of fine aggregate to one part cement and one part lime shall not be more than
(a)   five parts
(b)   six parts
(c)   seven parts

6   Explain the difference between 'co-ordinating size' and 'work size' of blocks.

7   Why should the bonding for fair-faced blockwork be carefully set out 'dry' before commencing actual building work?

8   Describe the method of ensuring that the courses of blockwork are kept level all round the structure.

9 Describe the problems that may be encountered when bonding partitions and buttressing walls into a main wall, and how these may be overcome.

10 What is meant by 'drying shrinkage' and how are the effects of this controlled?

11 State the treatment that should be given to openings formed in walls built in blockwork.

12 Describe how parapet walls may be built with blockwork.

Chapter 9

Openings in walls

After reading this chapter you should be able to:

1 Bond jambs and reveals in various bonds.
2 Understand various methods of fixing door and window frames to walling.
3 Install sills to window openings.
4 Have a good knowledge of various methods of bridging openings.
5 Understand how to construct precast concrete lintels.

Buildings have windows in order to admit light, and doorways to allow people to enter and leave. So much is obvious. But these openings form weaknesses in walls and if there happens to be any settlement or shrinkage of materials in the structure, then cracking is most likely to be seen where these openings are. This does not mean that cracking will *not* occur in a wall which has no windows at all and, in fact, shrinkage or settlement cracks are just as liable to occur in a mass wall, but because of the large number of joints, any cracks which do occur are so distributed that they become simply fine hair cracks and are not usually visible.

Modern architecture demands larger windows to let in maximum light; so it follows that if the area of walling is considerably reduced any cracking is distributed over a much smaller area, and so the movement will be concentrated and cracking will be clearly visible.

It is essential that you take care when forming openings in brickwork to achieve the greatest amount of strength and stability from the walling surrounding them.

Jambs and reveals

These may be of two types, square or recessed. The square reveals are easier to form and generally stronger. The amount of brick-cutting necessary to form the bond for recessed jambs tends to

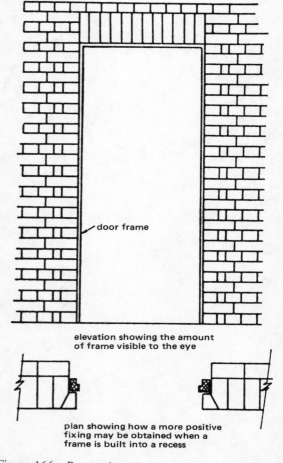

elevation showing the amount of frame visible to the eye

plan showing how a more positive fixing may be obtained when a frame is built into a recess

Figure 166 *Recessed jamb*

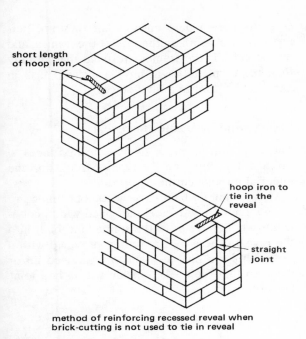

method of reinforcing recessed reveal when brick-cutting is not used to tie in reveal

Figure 167 *Recessed reveals*

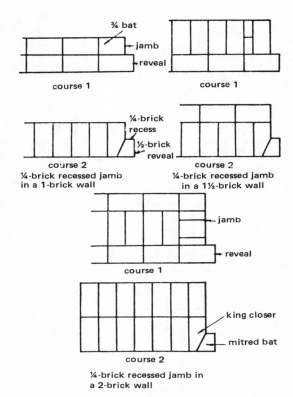

Figure 168 *Recessed jambs in English bond*

create a weakness unless a great deal of care is taken with the cutting.

Door frames with timber of large cross-sectional areas are set into recessed jambs so that the amount of frame which is visible to the eye is considerably reduced (Figure 166). This also gives greater rigidity to the door frame and provides a more positive fixing.

The principle of bonding at reveals is similar in all cases, but in Dutch bond it is necessary for rather more cutting than for English or Flemish bonds in order to *tie in* the reveal bricks to the wall. This cutting should not be difficult where a mechanical brick cutting saw is available. Where mechanical means of cutting are not available and cutting has to be done by hand, it is most likely that much will be left undone and reinforcement such as hoop iron can be placed from the reveal brick into the wall on every third or fourth course, as shown in Figure 167. Although the second method does not conform strictly to the *rules of bonding*, it nevertheless is economical and saves a lot of waste in labour and material.

The bonding for recessed jambs in various bonds is shown in Figures 168, 169 and 170.

Temporary fixing of frames

If the frames are to be built in the walling as the work proceeds, then the frames should be carefully placed in position, ensuring that they are at the right distance from the face of the wall, and then held in position by two boards (scaffold boards are quite suitable), nailed at the top and bottom, if possible. If the boards are resting on a concrete floor for example, then they may be held quite firmly with some bricks stacked at the bottom of the board. Two boards should be used, one at each end of the frame, so that if the frames are twisted then this twist can be taken out by adjusting the boards backwards or forwards as required.

Before the frames are built in they should be

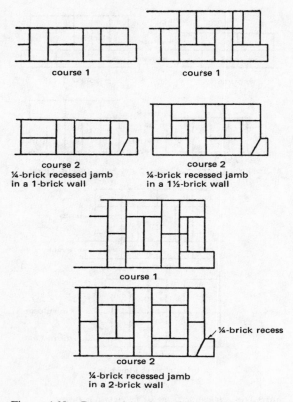

Figure 169 *Recessed jambs in Flemish bond*

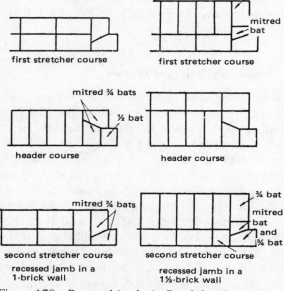

Figure 170 *Recessed jambs in Dutch bond*

carefully plumbed to ensure that they are perfectly vertical, both on the face of the frames, and on the side. If the frames are fixed inaccurately then the carpenters will have a difficult task in hanging the door at a later stage.

Fixing window frames to reveals

There are various methods of securing frames to reveals, depending on the type of frame and the material into which they are fitted.

Metal frames which have no timber lining are usually secured with steel lugs fixed with a countersunk bolt and nut to the frame, and built into the reveal. These lugs are often provided with a slotted hole to enable them to be moved up or down so that they will coincide with a bed joint (Figure 171).

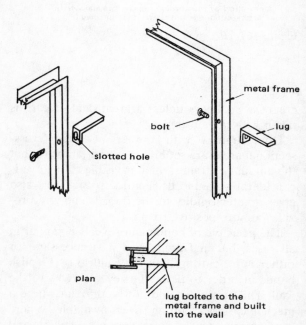

Figure 171 *Fixing metal frames*

If the metal window frame is fitted into a timber surround, then the metal frame should be bedded into the surround with non-hardening mastic, and screwed to the timber surround. The timber frame is then fixed by screwing galvanized iron cramps on to the back of the frame and build-

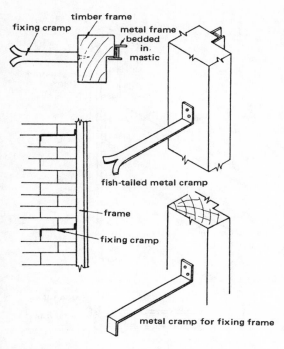

Figure 172   *Fixing timber frames*

1 Galvanized metal cramps similar to those shown in Figure 172 for fixing windows.
2 Building 100 by 75 by 6 mm wooden pads into joints of the reveal and then nailing or screwing the frame or lining into the pad. The pad should always be built in so that the grain runs parallel to the back of the frame, and the fixing is made across the grain (Figure 173). It will be a very poor hold if the wooden pad is built in so that the frame is fixed into the end grain as the pad is likely to be split by the screw or nail, whichever is used for the fixing of the frame.
3 Building breeze bricks into the reveal as fixing bricks, and nailing the frame direct into the breeze bricks.
4 Driving 150 mm nails into the back of the frame at course heights and building them into the wall. The advantage of this method, as with that of using cramps, is that no nail holes are visible in the frame aftyer it is fixed in position (Figure 174).

ing these into the brickwork. The ends of the cramps may be bent over or *fishtailed* (Figure 172).

If a metal frame is being fitted into a stone wall or a reveal which has stone dressings, and the courses do not coincide with the holes in the frame for the lugs, an alternative method of fixing may be used. Drill a hole in the stone about 12 mm wide and 75 mm deep, fill it with lead wool or a lead plug and fix the frame with a screw through the hole in the frame into the lead plug.

Door and window frames may also be fixed in walling by means of a plastic liner. A very efficient type of this lining is the Dactie plastic cavity seal manufactured by Econa Plastics (GB) Ltd, which not only provides a fixing for the frame but also seals the cavity. It is secured into the reveals by means of plastic lugs which are built into the walling.

Fixing door frames

Door frames may be of timber or metal. Timber frames may be secured by:

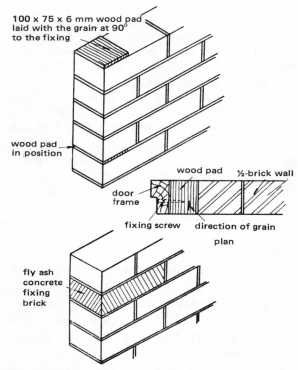

Figure 173   *Fixing timber door frames*

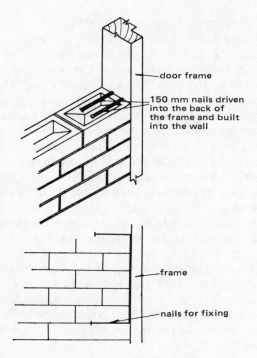

Figure 174   *Method of fixing frames in partitions*

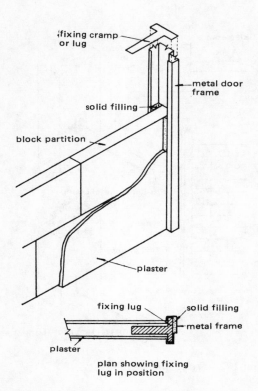

Figure 175   *Fixing metal frames in partitions*

Metal door frames are secured by lugs which are built in the wall, similar to those used for window frames. In addition you usually fill in solidly the hollow interior of the frame with mortar (Figures 175 and 176). The projection of the metal frame beyond the face of the brickwork makes it difficult for you to stretch a line between frames. This may be overcome by the use of a line guide (Figure 177), which is a steel clamp notched on one side for the line and having a thumbscrew on the other side for fastening on to the door frame.

Window openings

Window openings are provided with sills for two main reasons:

1   To give a finished appearance to the opening.
2   To prevent the walling below the window opening from becoming wet due to the absorption of water.

Sills may be of various materials such as stone,

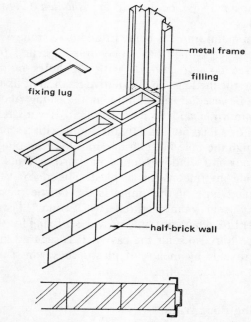

Figure 176   *Plan showing a metal frame suitable for a ½-brick wall*

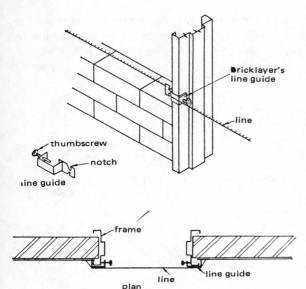

Figure 177 *Method of straining a line at the correct position on the face of the brickwork between steel door frames*

reconstructed stone-faced precast concrete, brick, tile, or hardwood timber, and some typical examples are shown in Figures 178–182. Always take special care with the construction of sills, so that

they do not allow water to reach the walling immediately below the opening.

Water can penetrate a building in two ways:

1 By capillarity, where the water travels through very small spaces or pores; or
2 By surface tension, where the water adheres to the sill and runs back to the wall, thereby causing it to become damp.

There are several points which should be noted when putting in sills.

1 The slope or *weathering* of the sill should be steep enough to throw the water off quickly.
2 A water bar or break in the joint under a sill should be provided to prevent capillarity.
3 Provision should be made to prevent water passing from a sill to the walling by means of surface tension. Figure 178 shows how water is prevented from reaching a wall by this means, causing dampness in the wall and possibly dry rot in the frame.

To prevent water from running off the face and along the underside of the sill on the walling immediately below, a drip or throating must be provided (Figure 179). If a tile or brick sill is used then sufficient slope must be given to prevent the

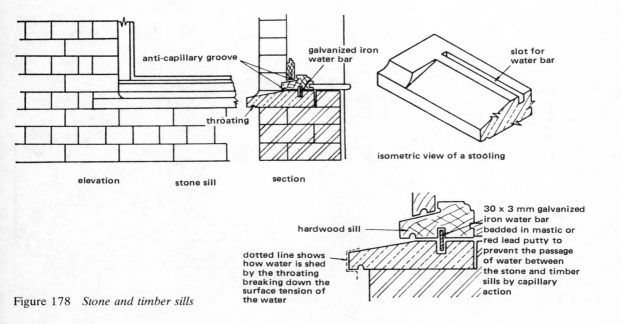

Figure 178 *Stone and timber sills*

water from running back to the wall. To act as a further safeguard against the penetration of water, particularly in cavity walls, a damp-proof course may be placed under and at the back of the sill (Figure 180).

Tile sills are usually put in after the frame has been fixed and built in. The lower course should be laid with the line fixed to the lower arris (Figure 181), and the top course laid with the line stretched to the upper arris.

An alternative method is to fix a piece of batten at the required height before laying the first course of tiles, spread the mortar behind the batten and bed the tiles in the mortar. The batten will keep the lower course straight and will also hold it firm and prevent it from becoming pushed out of place while the top course is being laid (Figure 182).

If the end of the sill is built into the reveal, this is called the *stooling* and examples of stone and tile stooling are shown in Figures 179, 181 and 182.

Bridging an opening

The simplest method of bridging an opening is by means of a single unit called a lintel (or lintol)

placed across the opening. When a lintel is used it has a tendency to sag, which means that the lower half is stretching, or is *in tension*, whereas the

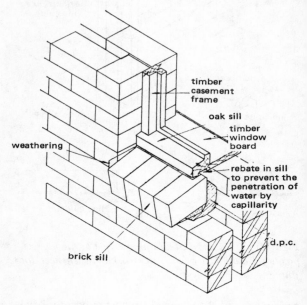

Figure 180   *A brick sill*

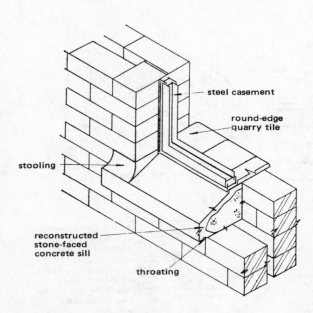

Figure 179   *A stone-faced sill*

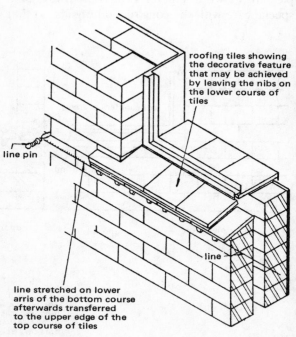

Figures 181   *Tile sills*

upper half is being squeezed in, or is *in compression*. The plane which is in the middle of the lintel is neither in compression nor tension; it is, therefore, called the *neutral axis* or *neutral plane* (Figure 183). The material used in lintels must be capable of resisting both compressive and tensile forces; the wider the opening then the greater will be these forces.

Wood lintels

These are satisfactory for bridging an opening provided that the timber is free from any large knots, splits or shakes.

One disadvantage is that they may gradually sag if constantly subjected to a heavy load. This can be overcome by building a relieving or discharging arch over the lintel (Figure 184). This type of arch should spring from each end of the lintel, so that the arch carries all the loading of the wall above the opening and transmits it to the piers on each side of the opening, while the small amount of brickwork between the lintel and the arch may be safely carried by the lintel with very little risk of sagging.

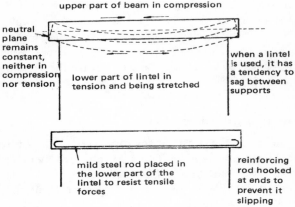

Figure 183　*Bridging an opening*

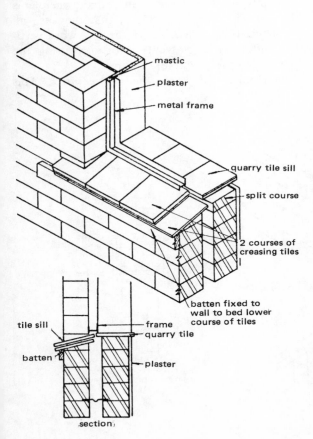

Figure 182　*Tile sills*

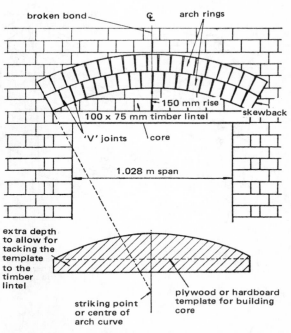

Figure 184　*Rough relieving or discharging arch*

This portion of brickwork infilling over the lintel is called a *core*. After the lintel has been placed in position, build up the core to the curve of a plywood or hardboard template which you should have cut to the shape of the curve of the underside of the relieving arch (Figure 184). Build up walling on each side above the opening and cut the skewbacks or sloping abutments and fix them to the correct slope. Then build the arch around the core, forming the curve by using *vee* joints between the bricks. When the first arch ring is laid and completed, spread a bed of mortar to an even thickness over the top ready to receive the second arch ring.

Reinforced concrete lintels

These are the most satisfactory type of lintel for bridging an opening. The steel reinforcement in the lower part of the lintel will accept (or resist) all the tensile stresses and the concrete in the upper part likewise the compressive stresses. A reinforced concrete lintel may be formed in one of two ways: casting *in situ*; or precasting.

Casting in situ. For this, formwork is con-structed across the top of the opening, the rein-forcement placed accurately in position, and the concrete finally poured and compacted in the formwork (Figure 185). With this method a cer-tain amount of delay occurs in the erection of the wall while the formwork is being erected and con-crete being placed and allowed to harden, but it is very suitable for larger lintels which are too heavy to lift by hand. It is important to remember never to underestimate the pressure created by wet con-crete, and therefore the formwork should be well-supported and securely fastened before fil-ling with concrete. The formwork should also be designed so that it can be easily dismantled with-out damage.

There are other methods of securing the sides of the formwork, for example, by using 'G' cramps which are specially designed for this pur-pose and are adjustable for quite a range of sizes of lintels, but they all have the same principle as that shown in Figure 185, in that they are all designed to keep the sides of the formwork verti-cal and rigid to prevent distortion during the pouring of the concrete.

Precasting the lintels before required. This

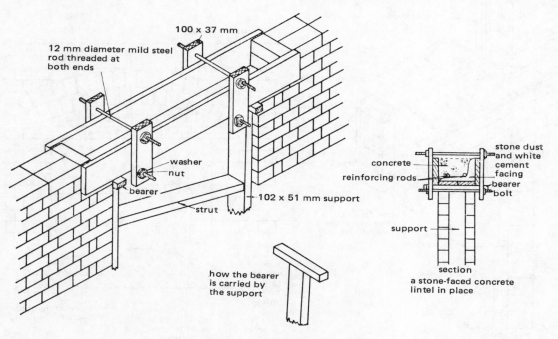

Figure 185 *Formwork suitable for* in situ *lintels*

method is far more convenient for small units than the previous one. As the casting is done at ground level the formwork (or moulds) need only be simple in design and can be used again many times. The lintels are completely set and hardened before use, and therefore there is little or no delay caused when building them into the wall. When lintels are cast the upper face should be clearly marked TOP so as to prevent the lintel being built in the wall upside down. If this should ever arise the steel would be in the upper part of the lintel and in this position could not provide the required strength. Since concrete is weak in tension, it is quite likely that even for a narrow opening the lintel would fail with the weight of the wall when it was built over the top.

Examples of designs of formwork for precasting lintels are shown in Figures 186 and 187.

In long lintels it is better to hook the ends of the reinforcing rods (Figure 183) to prevent the concrete sliding over the surface of the rod. This is

not likely to happen in short lintels such as those used for door openings.

One important factor must be kept in mind when precasting lintels: keep the weight of the lintel within the capacity of the men who are to

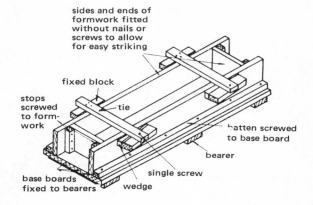

Figure 186   *Formwork suitable for precast lintels*

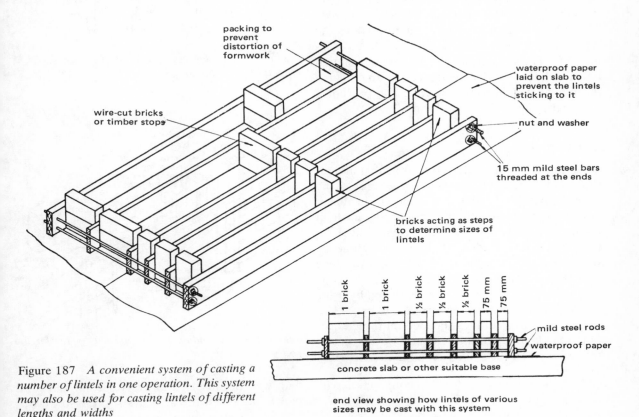

Figure 187   *A convenient system of casting a number of lintels in one operation. This system may also be used for casting lintels of different lengths and widths*

lift it, unless there is some form of mechanical lifting appliance on the site, in which case the size would be limited to the capacity of the appliance.

The mass of concrete is approximately 2402 kg/m³, and to calculate the mass of a lintel find the volume by multiplying the length, breadth and depth, using units of the metre, and multiply the answer by 2402 kg.

Example

Calculate the mass of a lintel 1.2 metre long, 0.112 metre wide and 0.15 metre deep.

Volume of concrete = $1.2 \times 0.112 \times 0.15$ m³
Mass of concrete = $1.2 \times 0.112 \times 0.15 \times$
$$2402 \text{ kg/m}^3$$
$$= 48.4 \text{ kg}$$

Reinforced concrete lintels made with ordinary Portland cement have a rather drab grey colour which may spoil the appearance of a wall which is built with face brickwork. For this class of work the concrete lintel may be stone-faced. This is done when the lintel is being cast by spreading on the soffit and face of the formwork a 25 mm thick layer of stone dust and white cement, before the reinforcement and the concrete are placed (Figure 185). The stone dust and white cement should be mixed to a stiff consistency, so that it can receive the weight of the concrete and prevent it from penetrating the stone facing.

Brick lintels

Sometimes these are referred to as soldier arches, though they are not arches in the true sense of the term. Brickwork is similar to concrete in that it has very little strength in tension; therefore it requires some other material, usually steel, to take the tensile loading. This may be done by supporting the brick lintel on a flat bar or angle iron (Figures 188 and 189).

A brick lintel may also be constructed by using perforated bricks (see Figure 2 on page 13), threaded on to steel rods, bedded on three edges of the brick, and pouring cement grout in each of the joints when the soldier arch is complete (Figure 190).

Brick lintels are often used in conjunction with concrete lintels. A timber centre is fixed across the opening and the arch can be built across this

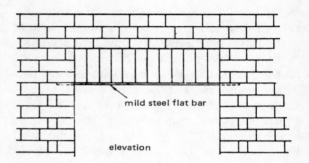

Figure 188   *Soldier arch or brick lintel*

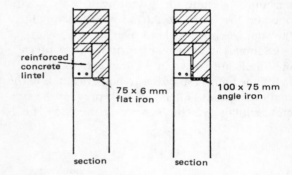

Figure 189   *An alternative method of supporting a brick lintel by using an angle iron*

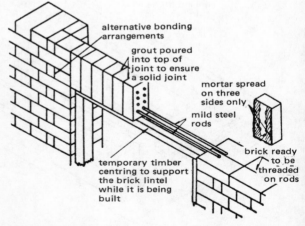

Figure 190   *A soldier arch supported by reinforcing rods*

with wall ties inserted in every second and third bed joint. When the arch has set, the formwork for the concrete lintel is made up and fixed in

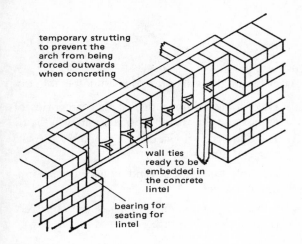

temporary strutting to prevent the arch from being forced outwards when concreting

wall ties ready to be embedded in the concrete lintel

bearing for seating for lintel

Figure 191 *A soldier arch built in conjunction with a reinforced concrete lintel*

position behind the arch. A support should also be provided on the face of the arch to prevent the concrete from pushing it out while it is being poured. The reinforcement is then placed in position and the concrete can be poured into the formwork and well-tamped around the wall ties protruding from the back of the brick arch (Figure 191). When the concrete has set it will provide a good support for the brick lintel.

When building soldier arches, take special care to ensure that the bricks are kept upright by using a boat level (see Chapter 3). If the bricks are not square then the joints should be kept truly perpendicular and the soffit as regular as the bricks will allow; this is most important as brick lintels or soldier arches look unsightly if the bricks are laid *out of plumb*.

Self-assessment questions

1   Wooden pads used for fixing door frames to walling should be
(a)   100 mm × 75 mm × 6 mm   laid   with the grain running at right angles to the back of the frame
(b)   100 mm × 75 mm × 12 mm   laid   with the grain running at right angles to the back of the frame
(c)   100 mm × 75 mm × 6 mm   with   the grain running parallel to the back of the frame

2   A 'throating' in a sill is introduced to
(a)   provide a decorative finish
(b)   prevent water from running from the front of the sill to the wall by means of surface tension
(c)   prevent water from running from the front of the sill to the wall by capillarity

3   When a lintel is placed across an opening, the lower part is in
(a)   tension
(b)   compression
(c)   neither in tension nor compression

4   A skewback is
(a)   a type of fixing for a timber frame
(b)   the slope of the weathering of a sill
(c)   the slope of brickwork cut to receive an arch

5   Creasing tiles are
(a)   special hard rectangular tiles with nibs used for sills
(b)   special hard rectangular tiles without nibs used for sills
(c)   special hard square tiles used for sills and flooring

6   Reinforcement for a concrete lintel should be placed
(a)   at the top
(b)   in the middle
(c)   at the bottom

7   The approximate weight of a precast concrete lintel 1.5 m long, 225 mm wide and 150 mm deep is
(a)   95.8 kg
(b)   121.6 kg
(c)   145.4 kg

8   Describe two methods of building in a tile sill.

9   Make neat sketches showing three types of sill.

10   What is meant by a relieving arch?

Chapter 10

Arches

After reading this chapter you should be able to:

1 Have a clear knowledge of the categories of arches and the various terms applied to them.
2 Have a basic knowledge of geometry for setting out arches.
3 Be able to set out and construct a semi-circular arch.
4 Have a clear understanding of the construction of an arch centre.

A more ornamental way of bridging openings is by the use of arches, which are comprised of small units bonded together around a curve or series of curves. (The term arch is derived from the word arc meaning part of the circumference of a circle.) Arches need no additional reinforcement, as brick lintels do, because the units are wedge-shaped, as a result of which the more load that is placed on an arch then the tighter will become the units in the arch.

Arches are generally classified into three main groups according to the use for which they are intended or the method of cutting and preparing the arch prior to its being built in position:

1 *Rough arches*, in which the *joints*, and not the bricks, are usually wedge-shaped. Such arches can be used on work which does not require a high standard of finish, or work which is to be plastered over. Little or no cutting is needed for this type of arch.
2 *Fine axed arches*, which are carefully set out, and the wedge-shaped bricks used are all cut to the same shape and size and have a pleasing appearance when finished. They are used on fine work and may be cut from the same bricks as the general face work, or sometimes bricks which have contrasting colour to the general work are used. This creates the effect of the arch standing out from the general walling.

3 *Gauged arches*, which are very ornamental and expensive as the bricks require a lot of preparatory work before they can be built in the arch and are only required for buildings of better quality. They are prepared and bedded with a very fine white joint, and a sound knowledge of geometry is required before attempting this class of work.

Arch terms

The following are a few of the more common terms used in the construction of arches (Figure 192).

The *voussoirs* are the individual wedge-shaped bricks in an arch.

The *span* is the distance between the jambs or reveals of the opening over which an arch is bridged.

The *soffit* is the surface of the underside of an arch.

The *springing points* are the lowest points of an arch from which the arch curve starts.

The *springing line* is a horizontal line drawn through the springing points.

The *rise* is the vertical distance between the springing line and the highest point of the soffit.

The *key brick* is the highest or central brick, usually the last to be built in an arch.

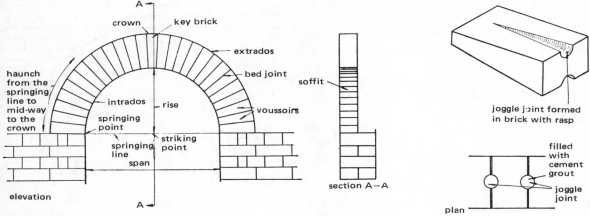

Figure 192   *A semi-circular arch*

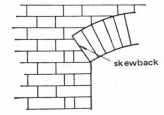

Figure 193   *Joggle joints*

The *crown* is the highest point of an arch at which the key brick is placed.

The *intrados* is the underside edge of an arch when seen in elevation.

The voussoirs for rough arches are usually set out on the intrados (Figure 184).

The *extrados* is the upperside edge of the arch as seen in elevation.

The voussoirs for fine axed and gauged arches are set out on the extrados.

The *haunch* is the name given to the lower part of the arch from the springing line to midway to the crown.

The *bed joints* are the joints between the voussoirs.

The *joggle joints*. In some cases when cutting arches, after the voussoirs have been cut to the shape required, a deep groove is cut into both beds, and if they are soft bricks then the joggle may be formed with the aid of a coarse half-round file (Figure 193). If hard bricks are used then the joggle may be gouged out with the aid of a scutch or comb hammer, or, preferably, they may be purpose-made. When the arch is being set, the joint is spread on three edges of the voussoir only – the bottom, back and front. After all the voussoirs are in place and checked for accuracy, then the joint core of each is filled with a strong cement/sand grout (1:1); when set, this forms a simple joggle joint.

The *face joints* are the cross joints in bonded

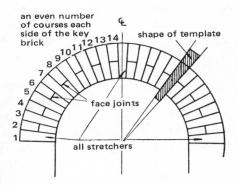

Figure 194   *This arch has the same span as the arch in Figure 192, but has been set out as a bonded arch. Therefore two more voussoirs have to be put in so that the springer brick and the key brick are the same*

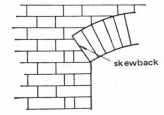

Figure 195   *Skewback*

arches, between the voussoirs in the arch courses (Figure 194).

The *skewback* is the name given to the sloping abutment from which an arch springs (Figure 195).

The *template* is the term given to a piece of material which is marked out from the full-size drawing of the arch and cut to the shape of the arch voussoirs. The arch bricks are then cut to match the shape of the template.

The *striking point* is the centre point from which the curve of the arch is drawn. In nearly all cases the voussoirs should radiate to the striking point or points of the arch in which they are being built. The voussoirs are then said to be *normal* to the curve of the arch.

The *label course* is any extra course built around the extrados of the arch, usually projecting on to the face giving it extra depth without cutting the bricks (Figure 196).

The *turning piece* is formed into the actual shape of the arch from a solid piece of wood. This supports the arch while it is being constructed (Figure 197). Turning pieces are generally used for segmental arches which have only a small span and rise. It is more economical to build up a centre from small pieces of timber when arches of dimensions greater than 1 m span and 75 or 100 mm rise are to be formed.

The *arch centre* is used for the same purpose as a turning piece – as a temporary support to carry the arch during its construction over an opening – but it is made up of a number of small-section timber members into the shape required (Figure 198). Arch centres have the advantage that they can be conveniently used over quite large spans. The timber members of a centre including the following:

Ribs: the shaped members which are formed to suit the required arch shape.

Ties: placed across the lower part of the centre to prevent it spreading out when it is carrying the weight of the arch.

Laggings: the small pieces of timber fixed across the ribs to carry the voussoirs. Centres may be open- or close-lagged, although open lagging is an inferior method to close lagging because of the difficulty in marking the position of voussoirs on the centre before building the arch. An alternative method is to use resin-bonded plywood nailed on to the ribs instead of the small timber laggings. This provides a smooth surface on which to work and is the most efficient method (Figure 199).

Bearers: the timbers which are fixed underneath the ties to prevent the ribs from spreading

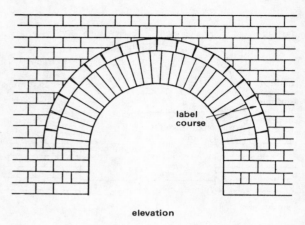

elevation

Figure 196   *Semi-circular arch with a label course*

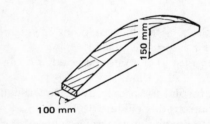

Figure 197   *A turning piece for a segmental arch made from two pieces of 100 by 75 mm wood nailed together*

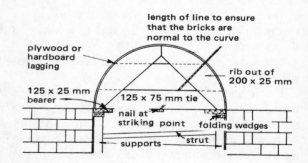

Figure 198   *A suitable centre for the arch shown in Figure 192*

apart. The bearers also carry the weight of the centre and arch.

Struts: used in larger centres to support the ribs off the ties.

Props: the main supports to keep the centre at its correct height.

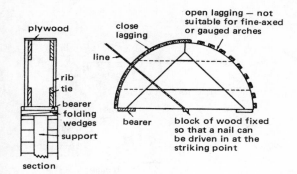

Figure 199   *A typical arch centre*

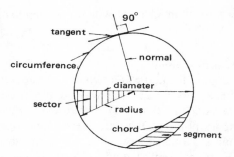

Figure 200   *Geometrical terms*

Folding wedges: placed between the props and bearers to provide any slight adjustment that may be necessary to the height of the centre before beginning to set the arch in position.

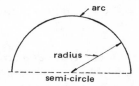

Figure 201   *The semi-circle*

The geometry of arches

Figures 200 and 201 illustrate terms which relate to various parts of a circle. All have some connection with the setting out of arches. A sound knowledge of geometry is most essential. See that you understand the following basic methods in order to carry out any work in connection with arch cutting.

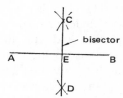

Figure 202   *Method of bisecting a line*

To bisect a line

The method of bisecting a line or dividing it into two equal parts is shown in Figure 202. When a line AB is the line to be bisected, open out the compasses to any distance greater than half the length of the line. First place the compass point on one end of the line at A and draw an arc above and below the line. Then place the compass point at B and using the same radius draw arcs above and below the line to cut the previous ones drawn at C and D. A line drawn through C and D will bisect the line AB at E.

To draw a line perpendicular to a given line

A line perpendicular to another line means that the lines meet at 90 degrees to each other, and the method used to bisect a line may also be used to draw a perpendicular. An alternative method however, is shown in Figure 203. To erect a line

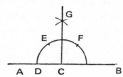

Figure 203   *Erecting a perpendicular line at a given point C*

perpendicular to a given line AB at a point C, place the compass point at point C and with any suitable radius draw a semi-circle; with the same radius place the compass point on D and draw an arc at E, and similarly from E with the same radius draw an arc at F. Place the compass point on E and using the same radius as for the semi-circle, draw an arc above point C; place the compass point at F and using the same radius draw an arc cutting the previous arc at G. A line drawn through G to C will be perpendicular to line AB.

To bisect an angle

An angle is formed when two lines meet at a point called a vertex, and the way to bisect such an angle ABC is shown in Figure 204. Place the compass point at B or the vertex and open the compasses out to any convenient distance and draw arcs at points D and E. Place the compasses at D and draw an arc within the two lines forming the angle; then place the compasses at E and using the same radius draw an arc to cut the previous arc at F. A line drawn through F to the vertex bisects the angle ABC.

To draw a tangent to a circle at a given point

A tangent is any straight line which touches the circumference of a circle at a given point (point A, Figure 205). This is perpendicular to the normal which also passes through the given point. Draw the normal so that it passes from the striking point of the circle through point A. Place the compass point at A and with any suitable radius mark off two points on the normal at B and C. Bisect the length BC by the method described in Figure 202, and the bisector DE is then tangential to the circle with its *point of contact* at A.

To find the striking point of an arc

Figure 206 shows how to determine the position of the striking point of a circle or an arc. Draw any two chords AB and BC in the curve, and then bisect them. Where the bisectors meet is the striking point of the curve. It makes no difference to the result if the chords are of the same or of different lengths.

Preparing the voussoirs for an arch

The following is an outline of the general procedure for preparing the voussoirs for a fine axed arch. This procedure may be slightly varied to suit the different arches but the basic principles remain the same.

1 An outline of the arch should be set out full size on a setting-out board.

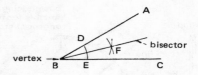

Figure 204   *Bisecting an angle*

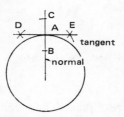

Figure 205   *Drawing a tangent to a normal*

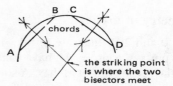

Figure 206   *Determining the striking point of an arc*

2 Mark out the voussoirs on the extrados of the arch. If the arch has a key brick then the voussoirs are set out by marking out the key brick first and dividing the extrados into a number of equal divisions which must not be greater than the width of the bricks being used plus the thickness of one bed joint. If the arch is to be bonded on face then there must be an *even* number of voussoirs *each side* of the key brick. This will ensure that the springing brick corresponds to the key brick (Figure 194).

3 When the common size of the voussoirs has been determined, complete the shape by drawing the joint lines between the extrados and intrados, so that they radiate to the striking point of the curve, thus ensuring that the bricks are *normal* to the curve (Figure 207).

4 Cut a template, which may be a piece of plywood or hardboard, to the shape of the voussoirs on the full-size drawing.

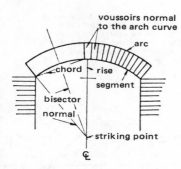

Figure 207 *A segmental arch*

One method of marking the template is to extend any two lines of the arch voussoirs, laying the plywood or hardboard between and transferring the lines to the upper surface by means of a straightedge. The template should be considerably longer than the depth of the arch, and should extend at the narrow end of the template (Figure 208).

5   Check the accuracy of the template shape against other voussoirs in the full-size drawing.

6   After the shape is checked the joint can be determined by laying a straightedge along one of the bed joints on the drawing, and placing the template against it so that it fully covers a voussoir. Then move the template along the straightedge until the required thickness of bed joint is visible on the drawing. Mark on each side of the template the cutting mark for the bricks. It is useful to nail a strip to the template at the cutting mark (Figure 209).

7   Mark the bricks by placing the template on the face of the brick (Figure 210). Mark the soffit with the aid of a square (Figure 212). Cut the bricks with the cutting tools illustrated in Chapter 3.

8   When the voussoirs are being axed, it is advisable to cut a joggle in the beds to allow for final grouting up when the arch is in place (Figure 211).

9   After completing the cutting of the voussoirs, secure the centre carefully in position; make adjustment as required with the aid of the folding wedges.

10 Mark accurately around the centre the posi-

tion of the voussoirs on the intrados and the width of the joints (Figure 212).

11 Drive a nail at the striking point(s) and attach a length of line so that the radiation of the bricks to the striking point may be

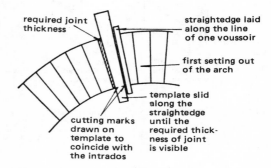

Figure 208 *Setting out an arch*

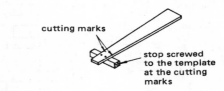

Figure 209 *A template for arch voussoirs*

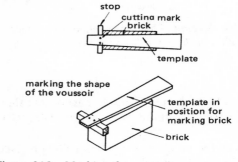

Figure 210 *Marking the voussoirs*

Figure 211 *Voussoir cut and joggled ready for fixing*

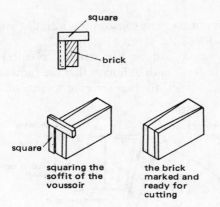

Figure 212   *Squaring the soffit of the voussoir*

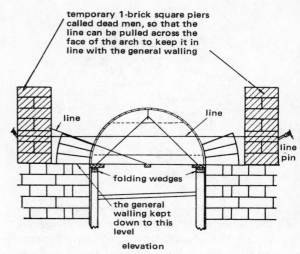

Figure 214   *Method of building in an arch with the aid of 'dead men'*

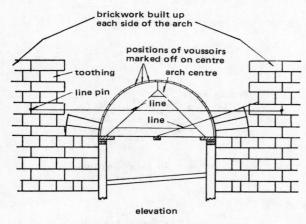

Figure 213   *Method of building in an arch by building up the walling each side of the arch first*

each voussoir for its correct position on the centre and correct alignment by means of the line from the striking point.

14   When the arch is finally in position, if joggles have been provided in the beds these may be filled with a strong cement and sand mortar (1:1 or 1:2 mix), poured into the joints.

Removing the centre

After the arch has been allowed to set, first ease the folding wedges allowing the arch to take its load gently, then remove altogether, and finally take out the centre and release the struts.

Self-assessment questions

1   Rough arches are those
(a)   whose joints are wedge-shaped and not the bricks
(b)   which are only approximate in shape
(c)   built by an inferior craftsman

2   The intrados of an arch is
(a)   the inside edge
(b)   the outside edge
(c)   the highest point

checked for accuracy and to ensure that they are normal to the curve (Figures 198, 213, 214).

12   Check the arch for straightness along its face (a) by building up the brickwork each side of the arch and stretching a line in between to line up the arch, as shown in Figure 213; or (b) by stretching a line between two temporary 1-brick piers erected each side of the opening. These are called *dead men* (Figure 214).

13   Build up the arch evenly on each side, meeting it at the middle or key brick, checking

3 The face joints are
  (a) the joints between the voussoirs radiating to the striking point of the arch
  (b) the joints between the voussoirs running parallel to the inside edge of the arch
  (c) the joints each side of the key brick

4 An arch centre is
  (a) the point from where the curve of the arch is taken
  (b) the centre line of an arch
  (c) the temporary wooden support on which the arch is built

5 A tangent to a curve is a line which
  (a) cuts the circumference at two places
  (b) touches the circumference at one point
  (c) runs from the striking point of the circle to the circumference

6 In a bonded arch, the number of voussoirs each side of the key brick should be
  (a) odd in number
  (b) even in number
  (c) it does not matter

7 A template is a
  (a) piece of wood cut to the shape of the required voussoir
  (b) solid piece of wood cut to the shape of the arch and upon which the arch is built
  (c) timber centre on which the arch is built

8 Draw to a scale of 1:10 the elevation of a segmental arch having a span of 1 m, a rise of 150 mm and a depth on face of 225 mm.

9 Describe the procedure for obtaining a template for a fine axed arch.

10 Describe the method of setting up the centre and building a semi-circular arch.

Chapter 11

Cavity walls

After reading this chapter you should be able to:

1 Have a clear understanding of the construction of cavity walls.
2 Know how to prevent dampness penetrating to the inner leaf of a cavity wall.
3 Know how to build foundations for cavity walls.
4 Know how to provide ventilation for rooms and hollow timber floors.

Walls may be built as solid walls, that is, having one thickness only, or cavity walls, being comprised of two walls (not necessarily of equal thickness), with a space in between. These walls are called leaves and are generally referred to as the outer leaf and inner leaf.

The space or hollow in between the walls has two main advantages:

1 When the outer leaf becomes wet the space prevents water passing from the outer wall to the inner wall, and thus the interior of the building remains dry.
2 The space will not allow heat to be transferred from one wall to the other. This arises from the fact that air is a bad conductor of heat and the cavity acts as a barrier. The cavity, therefore, is a good heat insulator and helps to keep the building cool in summer and warm in winter.

If the cavity is sealed at the base, eaves, and all the jambs of openings, then the air trapped inside will be static and this will ensure good heat insulation for the building.

The cavity may also be filled with an insulating material but this will be dealt with in more detail in *Brickwork 2*.

The size of the cavity

The cavity should be large enough to provide suitable insulation, but not so wide as to make it difficult to *tie* the two walls together – the Building Regulations state that the width of the cavity at any level should be not less than 50 mm nor more than 75 mm where suitable ties are placed at distances apart not exceeding 900 mm and 450 mm vertically.

A cavity may be not more than 100 mm wide if vertical twist-type ties are used and are placed at distances apart not exceeding 750 mm measured horizontally and 450 mm measured vertically.

Wall ties

These are used to tie the walls together, or to stabilize them. They are generally made of a non-ferrous metal or stainless steel, which are fully dealt with in BS 1243. Figure 215 shows various types of ties that are used in cavity walling; all types have one thing in common, in that they are designed to trap the passage of water from the outer to the inner leaf (Figure 216). This is an essential requirement if the cavity is to function properly and keep the inside wall dry.

The wall ties must be placed close enough together to ensure that stability in the wall is maintained. Building Regulations require ties to be placed at distances not exceeding 900 mm horizontally and 450 mm vertically.

In practice it is found to be an advantage if the ties can be *staggered* (Figure 217).

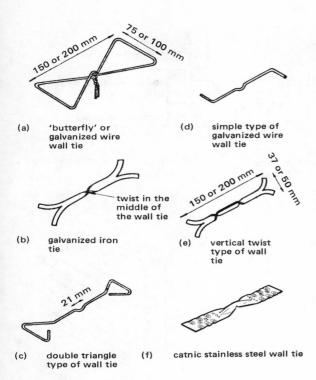

Figure 215 *Cavity wall ties*

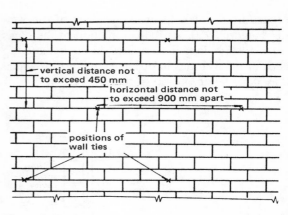

Figure 217 *Elevation of a cavity wall showing the wall ties 'staggered' throughout the wall*

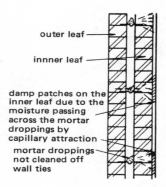

Figure 218 *Dirty wall ties can cause damp patches in a wall*

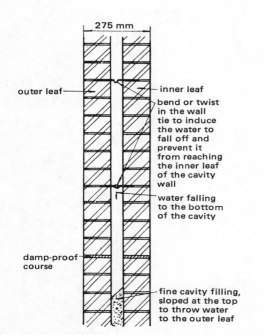

Figure 216 *Ties trapping the passage of water from the outer and inner leaf*

When cavity walls are being built it is essential that the wall ties be absolutely free from mortar droppings on completion of the walling, otherwise this can cause a *bridge* across the cavity which may allow water to pass across and cause the inner leaf to become damp (Figure 218). You can keep cavities reasonably clean and free from mortar droppings if you continually use cavity battens during the process of raising the work. Beginning at the lowest part of the wall, a length of batten is placed on the first level of wall ties to catch the mortar droppings as the cavity wall is built to the next level of ties. At this stage the batten is carefully raised, the loose mortar is cleaned off and returned to the mortar boards and the batten replaced on the new layer of wall ties. The same procedure is carried out at the level of the wall ties (Figure 219). At the completion of the day's work, insert a long battern into the cavity, and tap each of the wall ties to dislodge any mortar which may have fallen on top of them.

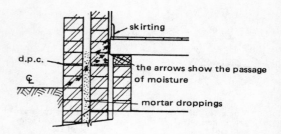

Figure 220 *How moisture can penetrate to the inner leaf and cause damage to a timber floor*

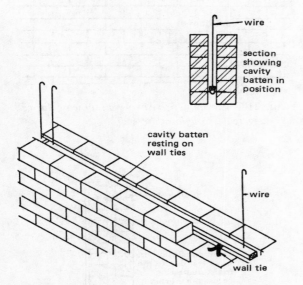

Figure 219 *Method of keeping a cavity clean during construction*

In a similar way the bottom of the cavity should be kept clean, and so that this can be done while the wall is built, cleaning holes should be provided at frequent intervals in the first course of the fair work above the cavity filling; this allows the cavity to be thoroughly cleared of mortar droppings. These holes are filled in by brick inserts after the wall is completed. If the mortar droppings are allowed to rise above the damp-proof course, the rising damp may penetrate the inner leaf and also the flooring, which may well be the prime cause of dry rot in a timber floor (Figure 220).

Damp-prevention in the cavity

Other places where dampness may penetrate to the inner leaf are at reveals, heads of openings and sills. Therefore a damp-proof membrane

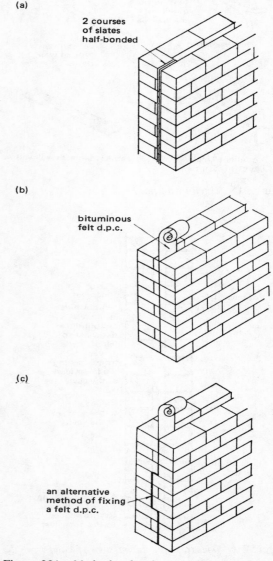

Figure 221 *Methods of sealing cavities*

should be provided at these points so that the interior will be kept as dry as possible. Figures 221–224 show methods of sealing the cavity at these places.

To give added stability to the two leaves it is also advisable to seal the cavity at roof level by bridging across the two leaves. Do this, however, above the level of the eaves so that it is then not necessary to insert a damp-proof course where the cavity is bridged at this level (Figure 225).

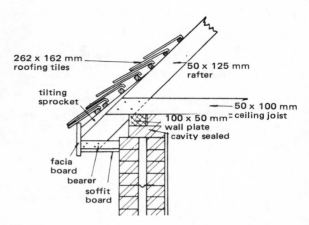

Figure 225 *Method of sealing a cavity at eaves level*

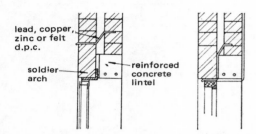

Figure 222 *Treatment at window heads to prevent dampness penetration*

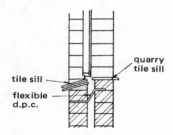

Figure 223 *Treatment at window sill to prevent dampness penetration*

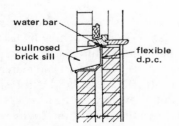

Figure 224 *Section showing typical treatment at a brick sill to prevent the penetration of water*

Foundations

Cavity walls for housing may be built directly off the foundation concrete; no footing courses are considered necessary, provided that the ground immediately below the foundations is suitable for carrying the load of the building. In these cases the cavity is usually filled with a concrete consisting of a small aggregate, not exceeding 10 mm, and cement, the mix of one part cement to six parts aggregate being suitable for this filling.

The filling is taken up to ground level and finished off to a steep slope, falling towards the outer leaf at the top. This slope will direct any accumulation of water which may collect inside the cavity away from the inner leaf. Water may enter the cavity when rain passes through the outer leaf, runs on to the wall ties, and drips off the middle of the ties into the cavity. Moisture may also develop from condensation, when the warm air in the cavity is cooled on the inside face of the outer leaf of the cavity wall. Warm air holds more water than cold air, so when the temperature of the air is lowered water is released in the form of droplets, known as condensation.

It is most important to dispose of this water as soon as possible and prevent it collecting in the base of the cavity, so in addition to the slope on the top of the filling, *weep holes* are left in the outer skin of the wall at the first course above the slope of the filling. The weep holes are formed by raking out the mortar in the prepend joints about

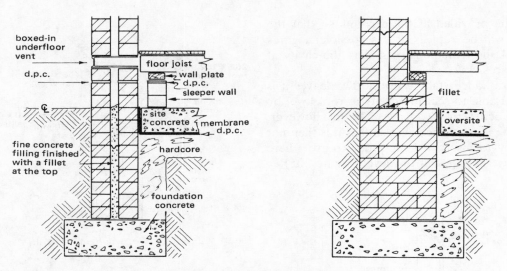

Figure 226   *Sections showing alternative methods of stabilizing the base of a cavity wall*

every metre along the wall. The joints should be completely free from mortar so that the water can drain away quite freely.

An alternative method is to build the wall solidly at the base and then begin the cavity at ground level, or at 150 mm below the damp-proof course, as shown in Figure 226.

Underfloor and room ventilation

Small openings, usually 225 mm long and 150 mm high, to ventilate the inside of the building, must be formed when constructing cavity walls. Such openings are necessary immediately above ground level to allow a free passage of air to the space under the timber floors, and at points above in the walls to ventilate larders, cupboards, lavatories, bedrooms and kitchens where gas boilers or heaters are installed.

These air vents through the cavity wall should be boxed-in with slates, which will ensure a direct draught to the space which is being ventilated.

For non-ventilated cavities it is essential to box-in all 'through' air vents, otherwise the advantages of these will be lost by creating draughts and will cause the cavity to become ven-

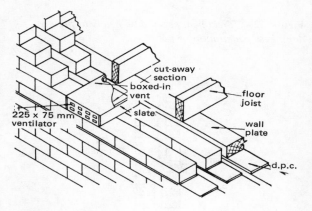

Figure 227   *Method of 'boxing in' a ventilator*

tilated. Figure 227 shows a typical method of boxing-in a 225 × 75 mm opening by using slates which are cut to the required size at the bottom, top and sides of the ventilator. The material used for boxing ventilators must be damp-resistant so that it will not allow any water to pass from the outer leaf to the inner leaf of the cavity wall. The same method can be used for a 225 × 150 mm or 225 × 225 mm opening.

Self-assessment questions

1 The cavity in a hollow wall
   (a) is a good conductor of heat
   (b) is a bad conductor of heat
   (c) makes no difference to the insulation of a house than using a solid wall

2 The minimum width of a cavity is
   (a) 50 mm
   (b) 75 mm
   (c) 100 mm

3 Cavity battens are used to
   (a) ensure the correct width of the cavity
   (b) collect any mortar droppings in the cavity
   (c) clean out the mortar droppings from the cleaning holes

4 The cavity should commence below the horizontal damp-proof course not less than
   (a) 150 mm
   (b) 225 mm
   (c) 300 mm

5 Water may penetrate to the inner leaf of a cavity wall by
   (a) travelling across the wall tie
   (b) travelling across any mortar which may rest on a wall tie
   (c) the air within a cavity

6 The maximum horizontal distance for placing wall ties in a 50 mm cavity is
   (a) 800 mm
   (b) 900 mm
   (c) 1000 mm

7 The maximum vertical distance for placing wall ties is
   (a) 350 mm
   (b) 400 mm
   (c) 450 mm

8 Explain why extreme care must be taken to keep a cavity clean.

9 Explain with the aid of sketches, methods of building reveals with square and recessed jambs in cavity walling.

10 By means of a sketch, show a typical method of 'boxing in' a ventilator.

Chapter 12

Pointing

After reading this chapter you should be able to:

1   Be able to compare the advantages and disadvantages of pointing as the work proceeds, with pointing after the walling is completed.

2   Be able to select suitable mortars and colouring agents for pointing.

3   Have a clear understanding of the procedure for pointing a wall.

4   Know the various types of pointing and the situations for which they are best suited.

Pointing is the term given to the final process of finishing a brick wall to give a neat appearance.

There are two ways in which walls may be pointed, and each has its own advantages and disadvantages. In the first case the mortar face joints of the wall can be pointed as the work proceeds, commonly referred to on site as 'jointing'. This is generally the more practical and the stronger method. In the second, the wall is built and then it is pointed after completion, and this generally provides a better appearance.

Pointing as the work proceeds

In this method a few bricks are laid and then the joints are pointed: this process is generally known as *jointing*. The number of bricks which can be laid will depend upon the degree of *suction* that exists in the bricks; the joint should not be too wet or too dry before pointing. It is quite common to complete each course and then point it in. The advantages of this method are as follows:

1   The face joints and the mortar within the walling are unified, so there is less possibility of the pointing being pulled out by frost action. Such damage by frost may be caused by water creeping between the pointing mortar and the normal bed of the bricks, then freezing and expanding. This expansion will force the pointing mortar away from the normal mortar

bed, eventually ruining the appearance and weathering properties of the brickwork.

2   It is the cheaper and quicker method of pointing because the wall is completed as it is being built, and no raking out of joints or refilling is necessary.

Its disadvantages are:

1   The difficulty of maintaining a uniform colour throughout the job unless careful watch is kept on the building sand which is being used on the site and the mixing of the mortar.

2   The difficulty of using contrasting coloured pointing mortar.

3   If it rains suddenly, the joints are difficult to point and there is a possibility of work being spoilt.

Pointing after the brickwork is completed

In this method the joints of the walling are raked out as the work proceeds to a depth of about 15 mm. A cavity wall tie is often used for this operation when the facing bricks are hard, but if the facings are of a soft nature, as, for instance, a hand-made sand-faced brick, then the use of the wall tie tends to take the arrises off the bricks. This has the effect of making the joints appear wider than they actually are, which can spoil a really fine piece of brickwork. In such cases it is

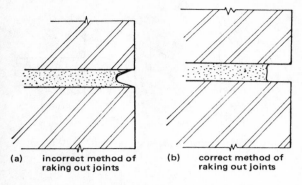

(a) incorrect method of raking out joints

(b) correct method of raking out joints

Figure 228   *Incorrect and correct way of raking out joints*

better to use a piece of wood sharpened down to the width of the joint.

After the joints have been raked out they should be well-brushed to remove any loose mortar and to ensure that the arrises are clean. The sections in Figure 228 show the correct and incorrect methods of raking out joints.

When the walling is completed, you should clean down with water. A scrubbing brush may also be useful for helping to remove obstinate patches or stains. The use of wire brushes should be generally restricted to hard facing bricks. Take great care if you find it necessary to use a wire brush on soft facings as the faces of the bricks can be spoilt with indiscriminate use of this type of brush.

When you have to clean down the wall it should be allowed to dry out because:

1   It is difficult to point a wall which is saturated because the face of the bricks may become soiled with pointing mortar.
2   The more water there is in a wall, the more shrinkage movement there is likely to be when it dries out. If this happens, then the bond between the bed joints and pointing mortar is liable to be broken when the first frost forces the pointing out of the joints, because the moisture trapped in the minute cracks will freeze, and, when ice is formed, will expand.

Ideally, a wall should be damp when you are pointing. In this state it achieves maximum adhesion and keeps shrinkage movement to a minimum.

Mortars for pointing

These vary in composition and colour according to requirements, but as a general rule the ultimate strength of the pointing mortar for a wall should not exceed the strength of the bricks with which the wall has been built. Hard, dense mortars can cause serious deterioration of some types of soft facing bricks.

For walls built with hard facings in exposed conditions a mix of one part of cement to two parts of sand may be used, but for general face work, a 1:3 mix is quite satisfactory.

Cement and sand mixed give a rather drab grey-coloured mortar, but if you substitute lime for some of the cement it can produce a lighter colour of cream or even a yellowish tint. If coloured mortars are required it is a good practice:

To mix all the pointing mortar dry in one batch;
    or
Ensure that sufficient sand is available for the whole of the work and that the ingredients are accurately gauged for each mixing. This is to ensure a uniform colour of mortar throughout the walling.

If you want other colours – black, green, blue, brown or red – you can get them by adding patent additives to the mortar. On a large site it is also good practice to gauge up various dry mixes until the required colour is obtained. If possible you should do this at least three or four weeks before the actual pointing operations start so that the colour of the pointing may be seen after it has set and dried. In fact it is quite usual for samples of walling to be built and pointed before beginning face work on some jobs. The gauge of the trial mix is then adopted for the rest of the pointing mortar for the site.

Pointing procedure

The mortar is carried on a hawk (see Chapter 3) and the joints filled in with a pointing trowel, using a small trowel for the perpends and a larger type for the bed joints. If the joints are to be cut, then cut one edge of each perpend with a trowel, and cut off the lower edge of each bed joint with a frenchman and pointing rule (Chapter 3).

For the usual method of pointing, fill in the perpends or cross joints first and when these are complete the bed joints are finished. Finally, apply a soft brush lightly over the face of the wall and remove any unwanted particles of mortar.

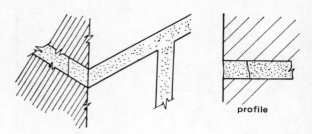

Figure 229   *A flush joint*

Types of pointing

Flush pointing. The mortar is pressed into the joint and finished flush with the brick surface (Figure 229). Sometimes a piece of sacking rubbed lightly over the joints makes them even, but you should turn or change it frequently or it will smear the facing bricks. This type of pointing looks extremely well with many types of hand-made facing bricks.

The *struck joint* is mostly used on internal fair-faced brickwork, and is carried out by striking back on the lower edge of the bed joint (Figure 230). In some isolated districts this type of pointing is done on external face work, but this is not good practice as water will collect on the upper arris of the bricks, and in winter this may freeze and cause spalling of the brick faces.

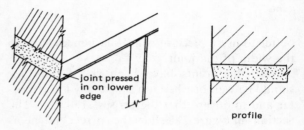

Figure 230   *A struck joint*

Weather-struck and cut. This is an excellent method of pointing for external face work, as it provides a good protection against the penetration of rain. The bed joints are pressed back on the upper edge of the joint (Figure 231). One edge of the perpends is cut and also the lower edge of the bed joints; thus where bricks of uneven sizes are used, the joints can still be made to appear all equal in width and straight along the bed joints. This type of pointing has a very neat and uniform appearance.

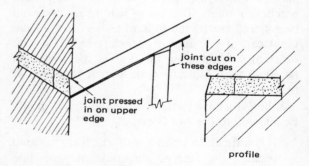

Figure 231   *A weather-struck and cut joint*

Rounded or *tooled pointing* is in some districts also called *bucket-handle pointing*. The joints are formed hollow by rubbing a jointing iron (Chapter 3) over them. This type of pointing has the advantage of being well-pressed into the joint, making it dense, and this looks particularly effective where the bricks and joints are of regular shape and size (Figure 232).

Recessed pointing is not very common, yet it looks most effective when it is done really well. It has a particularly pleasing appearance on internal face brickwork or on brick fireplaces, provided the bricks are of fairly regular shape and size. The

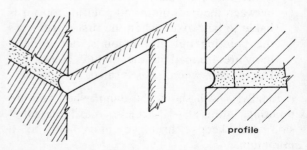

Figure 232   *A rounded or tooled joint*

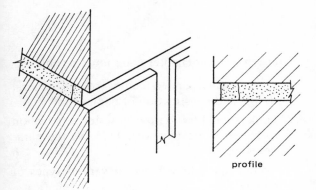

profile

Figure 233   *A recessed joint*

joints in the walling must be even in size. It is not recommended for external face work unless the bricks are of a hard dense sort. You form recesses by rubbing into the joints a brick jointer or a piece of wood planed to the same width as the joints (Figure 233).

Coloured pointing

This is a modern treatment for pointing. The different colouring agents which are available for mortar make possible a wide variety of pointing for face brickwork. For instance, cross-joints and bed joints may be pointed with contrasting colour. This gives the effect of having continuous lines across the wall and no visible perpends.

A variation of this type of pointing is illustrated in the monk bond shown in Chapter 3.

Pointing can play an important part in enhancing the colouring of bricks, but on the other hand an ill-chosen mortar colour can kill the colour in the brickwork, giving the wall a dead appearance, and it is just as well to erect specimens of work to see the effects before carrying out any major amount of work.

Self-assessment questions

1   'Jointing' is the term given when pointing
   (a)   after the walling is completed
   (b)   as the work proceeds
   (c)   with a special tool

2   The recommended depth to which joints should be raked out for pointing is
   (a)   9 mm
   (b)   12 mm
   (c)   15 mm

3   When pointing brickwork the walling should be
   (a)   dry
   (b)   damp
   (c)   wet

4   Gauging the ingredients for a pointing mix
   (a)   helps the mortar to be mixed more quickly
   (b)   ensures even colour of the mortar over all the walling
   (c)   makes for easier mixing

5   A struck joint is produced by rubbing it in with a
   (a)   trowel, striking back on the lower edge of the joint
   (b)   jointing tool
   (c)   trowel, striking back on the upper edge of the joint

6   Recessed pointing is particularly effective on
   (a)   external face work built with soft facing bricks
   (b)   fair-faced brickwork built with common bricks
   (c)   internal brickwork built with facing bricks

7   List the tools that are likely to be used when pointing a wall with weather-struck and cut joints.

8   What is the general rule regarding the ultimate strength of a mortar intended for pointing purposes?

9   State how coloured mortars may be used with advantages in pointing.

10   Describe how frost may affect the joints in a wall which has been pointed after the wall was built, and what methods may be adopted to keep such damage to a minimum.

Chapter 13

Parapet walls

After reading this chapter you should be able to:

1 Have a clear understanding of the general design and construction of parapet walls.
2 Understand how to prevent water penetration to the structure immediately below the parapet wall.
3 Have a good knowledge of various types of copings.
4 Be able to provide outlets in a safe and efficient way in parapet walls.
5 Have a clear understanding of corbelling brickwork.

Special care should be taken in the design and construction of parapet walls, because their exposed position makes deterioration likely.

The type of bricks for walls in exposed positions should be:

Hard-burnt or dense to withstand the action of frost, so that if any water which has soaked into the bricks freezes, it will not easily cause spalling of the face bricks.

Free from soluble salts such as sodium sulphate (Glauber salts) or magnesium sulphate (Epsom salts). Any rain which soaks into the wall will dissolve these salts and form a solution inside, and when this dries out the water evaporates into the atmosphere through the face of the wall, leaving the salts behind on the surface in the form of crystals.

Any high salt-content present in the bricks is likely to cause a concentration of crystals on or near the surface of the wall, and this will cause the effect commonly called *efflorescence*, which looks unsightly on face brickwork. When a salt solution reverts back to crystals it expands (just as water does when it turns into ice), and therefore, any concentration of salts which collects behind the surface of a brick may also cause spalling of the face due to the expansion of the salts. Hard-burnt

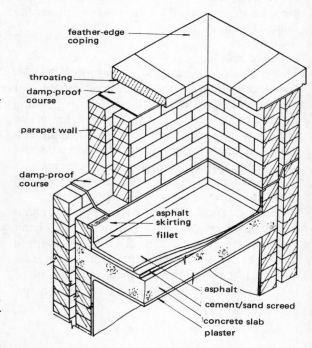

Figure 234 *An internal angle of a parapet wall and the method of keeping dampness out of a building*

bricks, especially, have to be strong enough to withstand this expansion, and to resist any spalling of the faces.

Parapet walls should be provided with a low-level damp-proof course to prevent water from penetrating downwards within the brickwork and into the rooms situated immediately below the roof (Figure 234). The various types of damp-proof courses may be of the same materials as those described in Chapter 6. A damp-proof course should also be bedded immediately below the coping to prevent the parapet wall itself becoming saturated.

Parapet walls should be protected on their upper surface against the effects of the weather by means of a coping. The following are four main points concerning copings:

1 They should have a weathering or slope on the upper surface to shed any rain quickly.
2 They should keep the water away from the face of the wall as much as possible.
3 The material for the coping should be capable of resisting the action of the weather.
4 They should give a good appearance to the top of the wall.

Copings

Brick-on-edge capping. This is a common type of finish but the bricks must be hard and preferably laid with a fall, as shown in Figure 235. Rough-textured bricks, especially the rustic facing brick, should never be used for copings because of probable frost damage. On thicker walls the bricks on edge should be bonded as shown in Figure 236.

Brick-on-edge and *tile creasing*. This has a better appearance than the brick-on-edge capping and also has the advantage of shedding the water away from the face of the wall (Figure 237). The tile generally used is the creasing or nibless type, though a very pleasing effect may be achieved if standard roofing tiles are used on the lower course with the nibs projecting downwards (Figure 238). The top of the tile creasing should be finished off on both sides with a cement and sand fillet. This is essential, otherwise water is liable to soak into the joint between the bricks laid on edge and the tiles, and in the event of freezing is liable to expand, thereby causing the brick-on-edge to be disturbed and loosened.

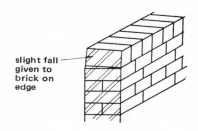

Figure 235 *Brick-on-edge capping*

Figure 236 *Bonded brick-on-edge capping for a 1½-brick wall*

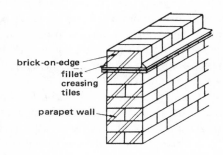

Figure 237 *Brick-on-edge and tile creasing*

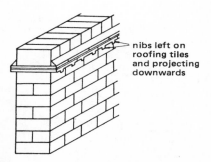

Figure 238 *Brick-on-edge and tile creasing using roofing tiles*

An important point when laying the creasing tiles is to make certain that the lower edge of the bottom course and the upper edge of the top course are laid to the line which ensures that these edges are parallel and straight.

Saddle-back coping. For walls of 1-brick in thickness, purpose-made bricks may be used to finish off the wall (Figure 239). These provide an excellent finish to a wall but do not throw any water clear of the face of it, so that staining is likely to disfigure the face work. An alternative method of constructing saddle-back coping is to form it in brickwork (Figures 240 and 241), but take great care when building this type of coping as the top and two front edges must be kept straight for the sake of appearance, and the bricks must be laid at a constant pitch or slope. The bricks forming this type of coping should be bonded, and the length of the wall should be carefully checked and the bonding determined before you lay the coping. This will ensure that the bonding continues unbroken throughout the coping; otherwise straight joints which look unsightly will occur in the middle of the coping.

Half-round coping. This is another type formed with special bricks similar to those described in Chapter 1. These bricks may be used with a tile creasing, or without. The former gives the better appearance and is more effective in keeping the water from the face of the wall.

Stone copings may be of natural stone or stone-faced concrete, and are laid on a mortar bed. Joggle joints should be used to prevent the stones from being easily lifted or displaced. Two common types of coping are:

1 Saddle-back (Figure 242)
2 Feather-edged or weathered coping (Figure 243)

The projections of all copings should be provided with a throating or drip on the underside of each overhanging edge to breach the passage of any water running underneath the coping and causing it to drop off before reaching the face of the wall.

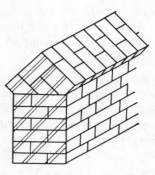

Figure 240   *A built-up saddle-back coping for a 1½-brick wall*

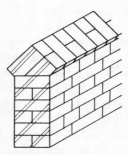

Figure 241   *Saddle-back coping built up with bricks*

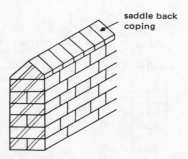

Figure 239   *Saddle-back coping using purpose-made bricks*

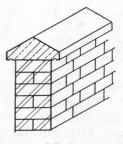

Figure 242   *A stone saddle-back coping*

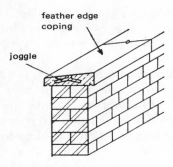

Figure 243   *Feather-edged coping*

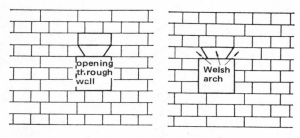

Figure 244   *Alternative methods of building a Welsh arch*

Outlets through parapets

Welsh arch

Often a small opening 225 mm wide by 225 mm high has to be formed in a parapet wall to permit water to run off a roof and pass through the wall into a rainwater hopper, which is usually fixed to the face of the wall below the parapet wall immediately underneath the opening. Such outlets must be carefully set out for bond. A Welsh arch is often used to support the wall above the outlet (Figure 244), though an alternative method would be to set a 450 mm long slate across the opening (Figure 245).

Oversailing courses or corbels

A corbel is the term given to a brick or series of bricks which project from a wall. Oversailing or corbelling work may be used to thicken a wall or form a decorative feature (Figures 246 and 247). When this type of work is carried out it is most important that the lower arris of each course be carefully lined up when laying, because this is the edge which is seen; any variation in the thickness of the bricks should be at the upper edge as it is less likely to be noticed. It is good practice to use header bond for corbels in which each of the courses projects a distance equal to a quarter of a brick; this gives the greatest strength to the corbel.

The Building Regulations state that the extent to which any part of wall overhangs the wall below shall not be such as to impair the stability of the wall or any part of it. This broadly means that no corbel shall overhang to such an extent as

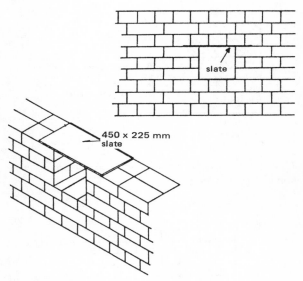

Figure 245   *Bridging a small opening by means of a slate*

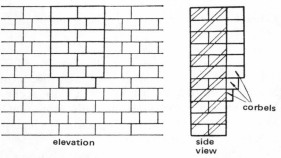

Figure 246   *A simple type of corbel forming a decorative feature*

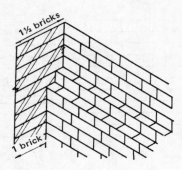

Figure 247   *A corbel used to thicken a wall*

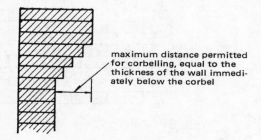

maximum distance permitted for corbelling, equal to the thickness of the wall immediately below the corbel

Figure 248   *Section showing maximum distance permitted for corbelling*

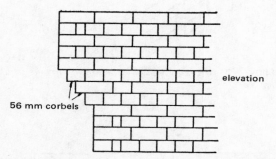

elevation

56 mm corbels

Figure 249   *Method of extending the length of a wall with 56 mm corbels*

and the other a 28 mm oversailing. The bonding is maintained as far as possible but broken bonds are bound to occur when this type of work is done.

Stopped-ends to brick copings. If a coping is to be finished with a stopped-end there is always a possibility of the end bricks of the coping becoming dislodged by frost action. To prevent this happening the usual method is to build wrought-iron cramps into the end of the wall and butt them tightly to the end brick (Figure 251).

Natural bracketing is the corbelling of a wall over a temporary opening which has been left to allow people to pass through while the building is being constructed. The bricks are corbelled with the bond and to enable the bricks to be built over the opening it is advisable to place two pieces of timber to support the corbels (Figure 252).

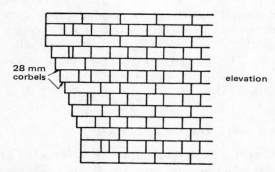

28 mm corbels

elevation

Figure 250   *Method of extending a wall with 28 mm corbels*

to cause the wall to be pulled over. To prevent the possibility of this happening, under no circumstances should a wall overhang a distance greater than the thickness of the wall measured immediately below the corbel (Figure 248).

Corbels may also be used at the end of a wall (Figures 249 and 250). One method has a 56 mm,

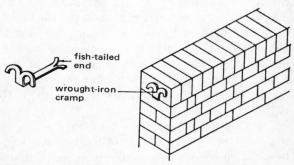

fish-tailed end

wrought-iron cramp

Figure 251   *Method of safeguarding the stopped-end of a coping with the aid of a wrought-iron cramp*

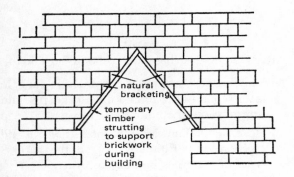

Figure 252 *Method of bridging a temporary opening in a wall with natural bracketing*

Self-assessment questions

1 Bricks intended for use in parapet walls should be hard-burnt in order to
   (a) carry the weight
   (b) stand up to people leaning on the walls
   (c) resist the action of the weather

2 A feather-edged coping is one which
   (a) has one sloping surface
   (b) rises in the centre and has two sloping surfaces
   (c) has no sloping surface

3 'Natural bracketing' is the term given to
   (a) a method of supporting a wall above an outlet in a parapet wall
   (b) corbelling the brickwork over an opening in a wall
   (c) forming a corbel for a knee at a gable

4 The bricks at the end of a brick-on-edge coping may be prevented from being dislodged by
   (a) using a stronger mortar
   (b) using a wrought-iron cramp
   (c) using reinforced brickwork

5 The maximum distance that a wall may generally be corbelled out along its thickness is
   (a) half of the thickness of the wall below the corbel
   (b) three-quarters of the thickness
   (c) equal to the thickness

6 State why it is desirable to use bricks which have a low sulphate content in parapet walls.

7 State the four main factors that should be considered in copings.

8 What is the purpose of providing a throating in a stone coping? Explain how the throating works.

9 Make a neat sketch of a Welsh arch.

10 What are the main points to consider when building oversailing courses?

Chapter 14

Partitions

After reading this chapter you should be able to:

1 Understand the type of construction suitable for a separating wall and how to keep sound transmission to a minimum.

2 Have a good knowledge of the setting out and erection of partition walls and the various types of materials in their construction.

3 Know how to make provision for the fixing of joinery, cutting holes for piping, etc., and fixings for brackets, etc.

Separating walls

A wall which separates two dwellings such as in a block of terrace houses or a dividing wall in a pair of semi-detached houses is termed a separating wall. The term 'separating wall' indicates that the wall is jointly owned by the owners of the two houses. The minimum thickness for such a wall should not be less than 190 mm or 1-brick.

It has been found that solid separating walls allow a great deal of noise to travel from one dwelling to another (Figure 253). Excessive noise passing through a separating wall can cause a great deal of annoyance and even mental suffering, and a lot of investigation has been carried out in recent years to attempt to find ways of preventing sound passing through walls, and of reducing it to the minimum.

One answer to this problem is to make walls as heavy as possible, as weight is the best sound barrier, but to soundproof fully would mean a wall about 600 mm in thickness. This is impracticable in modern building, so other methods must be adopted which are not quite so effective as sheer weight but which nevertheless reduce the amount of sound passing through the wall.

Separating walls may be built in a cavity construction, each 'skin' being ½-brick in thickness with a 50 mm wide cavity between. They may be built of bricks, dense or lightweight concrete, or

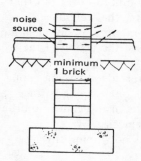

Figure 253 *Section showing how sound is transmitted through a solid separating wall*

hollow blocks. They should be built discontinuous as far as possible; for example, if wall ties are required to be used in the wall then less sound will be transmitted through the 'light' type of wire wall tie such as the 'butterfly' or 'double triangle' pattern than through the heavier ties of twisted steel. The cavities should also be kept completely free from mortar droppings as these will form a bridge for the sound to pass from one skin to the other. This type of wall should also be kept discontinuous from the main structure by (1) inserting layers of bituminous felt and (2) not sealing the ends of the cavity.

1 If the wall is to be built directly off the oversite concrete then the two skins should be

separated by a layer of bituminous felt built in at the base of the wall (Figure 254).

When the separating wall is constructed from its own strip foundation then the oversite concrete or solid floor should be insulated from the wall with a felt strip (Figure 255).

If a solid separating wall is required in the roof space, then there should be a bituminous felt strip provided between the cavity wall and the solid wall (Figure 256).

2 The cavity should be kept open at the ends where it meets the external wall by bonding the walls (Figure 257). This allows maximum stability with a discontinuous structure.

It is better if floor joists are laid parallel to the separating walls (Figure 258), but where this is not possible and the joists have to rest on the separating wall, they should be cut so that they do not have more than 112 mm bearing, and there should be a minimum of 112 mm between any two such joists built into a separating wall (Figure 259). This not only prevents sound-transmission but also complies with the Building Regulations concerning fire prevention in buildings.

Another modern method of giving end support for floor joists up to a separating wall involves the use of metal joist-hangers. These are pressed-steel brackets which are built into the wall so that the joists rest on the platforms formed in the brackets (Figure 260).

Partition walls

Walls separating rooms are called partitions and may be generally classified as load-bearing, and non-load-bearing, depending on whether they carry any weight other than their own, for example, if the floor joists rest on a partition wall then it would be classified as a load-bearing partition.

Lightweight materials are widely used for the construction of partitions. This reduces the total weight to be carried by the floors or slabs upon which the partitions are built. The lighter material also allows for larger units to be made, which can be handled quite easily. This means that partitions built with larger blocks may be built faster than if ordinary bricks are used.

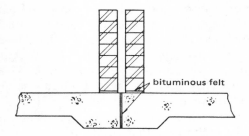

Figure 254   *Section showing a method of insulating a continuous slab against the transmission of sound by the structure*

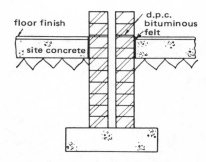

Figure 255   *Section through a cavity separating a wall*

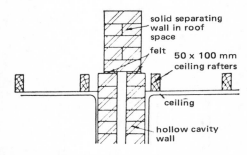

Figure 256   *Cavity separating wall reduced to a 1-brick wall in a roof space*

The following are some of the more common types of materials which are used for partitions.

Cellular fletton bricks. Lightweight fletton bricks which have large hollow recesses (Figure 261). These bricks are laid with their recesses downwards on the mortar bed to make certain that they are kept hollow and free from mortar.

Fly ash blocks. Made as lightweight slabs from a mixture of fly ash and cement. They are rough-textured and form an excellent key for plaster. Their nominal length is usually 450 mm and height 225 mm, thicknesses vary from 37 to 100 mm. They generally have a nib at one end and a groove at the other so that a joggle is formed at each joint (Figure 262). Fly ash blocks are very good for thermal insulation.

Foamed concrete blocks. Lightweight blocks made from cement and sand, aerated with an additive, creating air bubbles and making the block light in weight and less dense.

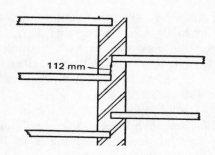

Figure 259   *Plan showing positions of joists if they have to be built in a separating wall*

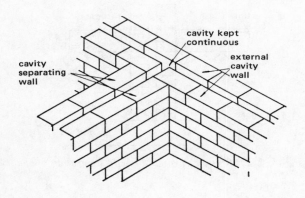

Figure 257   *A cavity separating wall*

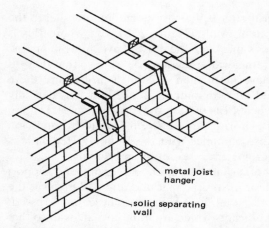

Figure 260   *Method of supporting floor joists on a separating wall by means of metal hangers*

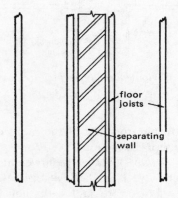

Figure 258   *Plan showing the floor joists running parallel with the separating wall*

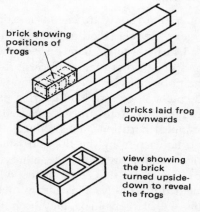

Figure 261   *Cellular fletton wall*

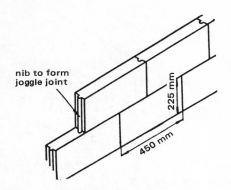

Figure 262   *Fly ash block partition*

Similar blocks are made with aluminium powder added to the mortar, which then expands and traps air in the block, making it into a lightweight unit.

Hollow terra-cotta blocks. Made from a finely washed clay with certain special properties, which is pugged and forced through an extruding machine, in the process of which the blocks are cut off to length as the continuous length of clay emerges from the machine. The thickness of the walls of the block is about 12 mm, which allows the block to dry quickly and thoroughly. The green clay blocks are then burnt at a high temperature. The partition blocks after firing are usually 300 mm long by 225 mm high and the thickness ranges from 37 to 100 mm for partitions. They may be smooth-faced for work which is to remain exposed, or grooved to form a key for plaster (Figure 263). These blocks are not very easy to

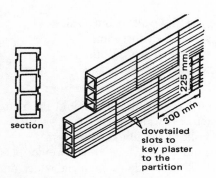

Figure 263   *Hollow terra-cotta block partition*

cut, so the manufacturers make special half-units so that the bond can be formed without actual cutting of the blocks.

As partitions are usually quite thin, from 50 to 100 mm wide, great care must be taken to ensure that they are well-bonded at angles and intersections; also, any pinning up to ceilings should be solid, so that the greatest amount of stability may be achieved.

During the building of thin partitions it is a good plan, whenever possible, to provide extra support by erecting profiles in the form of vertical timbers, say of 75 by 50 mm section (an ideal size), at corners and intersections by wedging between floor and ceiling with the aid of folding wedges (Figure 264). Where the partition walls are attached to main walls they should be block-bonded to gain the maximum stability (Figure 265). See also Chapter 7.

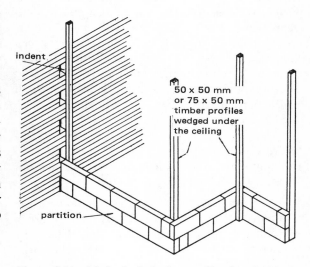

Figure 264   *Method of placing profiles for partitions*

Provision for fixing joinery

Skirtings and picture rails may be secured by either building fly ash blocks into brick walls, or by using special terra-cotta fixing blocks at the appropriate course in the hollow terra-cotta block partition. Architraves, door linings and frames may also be fixed to similar blocks built into the jambs of the opening formed. Fly ash block partitions need no special fixing bricks, as nails

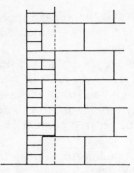

Figure 265   *Section showing the block-bonding of a partition into a main wall*

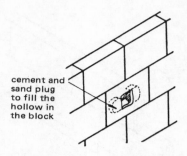

Figure 267   *Preparing a hole in a hollow block partition to receive a bracket*

may be driven into this type of block with little danger of damage.

Cutting holes for pipes

When holes for pipes are to be formed through partitions, those up to 37 mm in diameter may be cleanly and very rapidly cut with the aid of a tungsten-carbide-tipped drill, but larger holes must be cut by hammer and chisel from both sides of the wall. If an attempt is made to cut from one side only, then the opposite side is likely to spall badly, particularly in terra-cotta blocks.

Fixing cantilever brackets

In fixing these brackets in solid partitions such as fly ash type, follow this procedure:

1   Cut a neat hole with the aid of a club hammer and chisel for the bracket, only slightly larger than the bracket. The chisel should be kept sharp; a blunt chisel only creates extra work.

2   Brush out and dampen hole.
3   Fill the hole with a rich cement mortar (1:2).
4   Insert the bracket and support on the front edge with a slotted strut (Figure 266).
5   Tighten up the bracket by inserting a small piece of damp brick into the mortar each side of the bracket.
6   Ensure the bracket is at its correct level.
7   Allow the mortar to set.

When fixing this type of bracket in a hollow block partition, after the hole for the bracket has been cut, fill the cells solidly inside the block with cement mortar (Figure 267), and allow to set hard. Then the same procedure as listed above may be used.

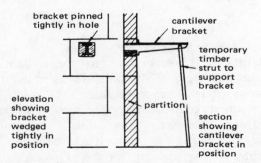

Figure 266   *Fixing a cantilevered bracket*

Self-assessment questions

1   A 'separating wall' is one which
   (a)   separates two rooms
   (b)   separates two dwellings
   (c)   separates two gardens

2   The best way to prevent sound from travelling across a wall is to
   (a)   build it in lightweight concrete
   (b)   render its surface in lightweight plaster
   (c)   build it in a dense material which makes it very heavy

3   The minimum thickness of a separating wall is
    (a)   190 mm
    (b)   200 mm
    (c)   212 mm

4   What is the difference between a separating wall and a partition wall?

5   Why should floor joists not be placed end-to-end in a separating wall?

6   What advantage has a hollow separating wall over a solid one?

7   How is the stability of partition walls ensured?

8   How may provision be made for fixing skirtings in partitions built with
    (a)   bricks
    (b)   fly ash blocks
    (c)   terra-cotta blocks

9   Describe the method of cutting a 100 mm diameter hole in a terra-cotta block partition.

10   Describe the method of fixing a bracket in
    (a)   a brick wall
    (b)   a terra-cotta block partition

Chapter 15

Concrete floors and roof slabs

After reading this chapter you should be able to:

1 Have a sound knowledge of the laying of concrete floors.

2 Be able to compare the advantages and disadvantages of providing a floated surface to a concrete slab, to providing a screed.

3 Have a sound knowledge of the method of laying a screed on a concrete slab.

4 Understand the advantage of using lightweight aggregates in floor screeds.

5 Have a sound understanding of the method of laying screeds, including setting up the battens.

6 Know how to lay a granolithic floor by a monolithic method; and a separate method.

7 Know how to lay a quarry-tiled floor; a wood-block floor; and a PVC tile floor.

Concrete slabs which are not required to be laid to falls but are laid level, such as for ground floors, should be finished with a floated surface so that the floor finish need not be applied to a screed placed as a second operation, but can be laid directly on to the slab. This is a more satisfactory method than laying screeds which are liable to become detached from the base concrete and cause failure through cracking or through lack of adhesion which may give a hollow sound when the floor is walked on.

A screed is a thin layer, usually about 25 or 37 mm in thickness, consisting of cement and washed sand in the proportion of about 1:3, and is laid on the surface of a concrete slab in order to produce an even surface ready to receive the floor finish. Screeds also have a particular use when concrete is used to form slabs or flat roofs which are required to shed water; it is usual for a screed to be laid on the top to render the surface even so that the finish can be spread on top of the screed at an even thickness. In the case of roofs the

screed would be laid to fall so that rain water could be drained off. The cost of finishes is usually high so it is more economical to make up falls with a cheaper material, keeping the finishing material to an even thickness.

In some cases the screed may be laid to serve as the floor or slab finish. The topping is said to be laid monolithically with the base concrete if it can be laid within three hours after the base concrete is laid. In this way you ensure a good key between slab and screed. Site conditions, however, very often make it difficult to lay screeds so soon after the concrete is laid, and the 'separate' method of laying screeds will be used. This way you should clean off the concrete slab very thoroughly, remove any laitance or scum on the top of the concrete and hack the surface well with a hacking hammer or mechanical hammer. Clean off finally.

Wet the surface well and allow the surplus water to evaporate. The slab then expands a little, so that after the screed has been laid and is hardening, the slab and screed shrink together, help-

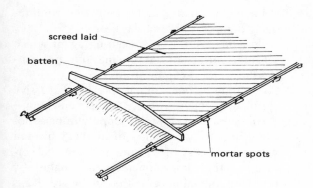

Figure 268 *Method of laying a floor screed*

ing to prevent the screed becoming detached from the concrete base.

The surface should be only damp when the screed is laid so that there is no surplus water to make the mix too wet, as this would make the screed weak and leave the surface dusty under wear. Using this method, the thickness of the screed should be about 37 mm.

To lay the screed, first put down timber battens to the required levels and pour a solution of cement and sand grout thinly over the slab. Then scrub it into the concrete base. This helps to give the screed extra key to the concrete slab. Spread the concrete or mortar in between with a shovel and then compact and bring to an even surface with the aid of a straightedge pulled along the battens (Figure 268). Then finish off the surface with a wooden float or steel trowel for whichever type of finish you want.

Heat insulation

If you use a lightweight material as the aggregate in the screed, it will mean better heat insulation and help prevent the warmth escaping from the inside of the building. All these lightweight materials have one main characteristic in common: they all contain a greater volume of air pockets or voids. Since air is a bad conductor of heat – provided that it is kept stationary – then the more air that is trapped in the screed the better will be the insulation. However, this type of screed is rather weak and therefore can only be used where a hard

finish is being used on the surface to protect it.

Lightweight materials that provide an excellent aggregate for these types of screeds include the following:

Foamed slag, a product which is formed by immersing molten slag from steel furnaces directly into water. The violent action of the steam on the slag, in a period of rapid change from liquid to solid, froths up the slag and leaves it full of air pockets.

Expanded clays, which release certain gases when heated to a high temperature; these gases expand the clay and leave pockets or voids in the material.

Exfoliated mica, a very light material, produced by heating mica and causing the layers to separate, leaving air spaces in between.

Sintered fly ash pellets, which are produced by mixing fly ash with a little water in large revolving drums and heating so that it forms into pellets which are then passed through sieves to grade them into different sizes.

Setting battens

Before placing a screed, timber battens should be laid to required levels. These are bedded on mortar pats and levelled with a straightedge and a spirit level (Figure 269).

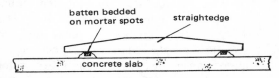

Figure 269 *Straightedge pulled along the tops of the two battens*

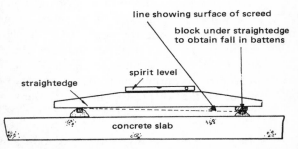

Figure 270 *Method of obtaining a fall in a floor screed*

If a fall is required in the screed, this is pre-determined and small blocks are made to rest under one end of the straightedge (Figure 270). The size of the block may be calculated according to the fall required, and the length of the straightedge that is used:

$$\frac{\text{fall}}{\text{length}} \times \frac{\text{length of straightedge}}{1}$$

For example, if a fall of 40 mm in 3 m is required and the straightedge is 2.25 m long, then the fall in 2.25 m will be:

$$\frac{40 \text{ mm}}{3\text{m}} \times \frac{2.25 \text{ m}}{1} = 30 \text{ mm}$$

The battens should be carefully checked for accuracy before laying the screed as it would be very costly to correct a screed which had been laid to an incorrect fall.

Floor finishes

Granolithic flooring
There are two methods of laying this type of finishing to a floor: monolithic; and separate. Wherever possible use the monolithic treatment in preference to the separate method, as in the former the maximum bond between topping and base is produced.

1 *Monolithic method*. Lay the topping within three hours of laying the concrete slab. The mix should be composed in proportions of 1:1:2 by weight of cement:fine aggregate:coarse aggregate. The amount of water should be just sufficient to obtain a workability that allows the topping to be fully compacted. Generally, it should not exceed about 0.45 by mass of cement. The topping should have a minimum thickness of 18 mm. About two hours after the topping is laid and fully compacted trowel it to a smooth finish. Under no circumstances should dry cement be used to absorb any surplus moisture which may be on the surface of the topping. Cure the topping by:

Spraying water over the surface as soon as it is hard enough to be treated;

Laying hessian and keeping this continuously damp for several days; or

Spraying with a patent curing agent which seals the surface of the topping, thus preventing the water escaping from it.

Avoid rapid drying out to prevent excessive shrinkage, which is likely to cause cracking.

2 *Separate method*. Lay the topping in bays not exceeding 15 m² super – of about 5 by 3 m with a thickness of 37 mm. Prepare the surface of the base concrete thoroughly by removing the laitance so that the aggregate is exposed, and brush and water the surface well, removing any surplus water before grouting. The grout should be composed of cement made into a stiff slurry with water and should be brushed over the surface of the concrete immediately before the topping is laid; this will provide a key or bond between the topping and the base. The surface should be trowelled and cured in the same way as for monolithic construction.

Quarry tiles
These are a very hard type of floor tile normally of face size 150 by 150 mm and 12 or 15 mm thick, available in red, brown, blue and buff colour. They form an excellent hard-wearing, waterproof surface. They may be laid half-bond or with

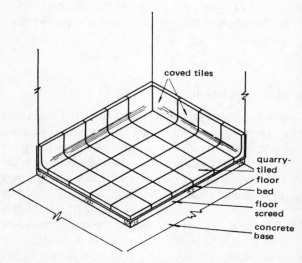

Figure 271 *Quarry-tiled floor laid with straight joints*

straight joints, with a skirting of coved tiles sometimes used to dress the tiled area to the walls
(Figure 271). Before tiling, lay a 12 mm thick
screed to the required levels and then bed the tiles
on top of the hardened screed in a cement and
sand mortar (1:3), and lay them to an even surface. The tiles are pointed after the floor has been
laid and when set the surfaces of the tiles are
cleaned off with cloth pads, as soon as possible
after completion. Any mortar stains which may
have been carelessly left on tiles are usually difficult to remove.

The richness of the coloured tiles may be shown
to the full by wiping the surface with a rag soaked
in a solution of one part linseed oil and two or
three parts turpentine.

Wood-block floors
Lay a screed of cement and sand 12 or 18 mm
thick to an even surface ready for the wood blocks
and allow it to set hard and dry out thoroughly.
Heat pitch mastic and apply while hot to the surface of the screed and spread quite thinly. Dip the
bed of each block before laying into a bucket of
hot pitch mastic and bed it on the layer of pitch
which is spread over the screed. Sand and polish
the floor for a smooth, even, finished surface.

Two common methods of bonding the blocks
are shown in Figures 272 and 273. One shows a
herring-bone bond and the other a basket-weave
bond.

Plastic, rubber and linoleum floor tiles
All these types of floor finish require a good finish
to the concrete base or the floor screed. Because
of the thinness of the tiles, any irregularity in the
surface will show up in the surface of the tiles.

All these tiles are bedded down in an adhesive
of one kind or another, and some tiles are
warmed before laying while others are laid cold.
In each case follow the manufacturer's instructions carefully. Failure to do this may result in
faults developing in the floor finish, such as the
lifting of the tiles off the screed, or deterioration
in the tiles through using incorrect bedding material. Certain types of solution must be left spread
on the surface of the screed for some time before
the tiles are laid on it. These are called emulsions.

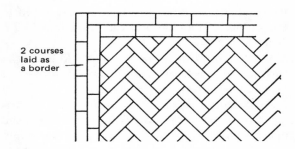

Figure 272　*Wood-blocks laid in herring-bone bond*

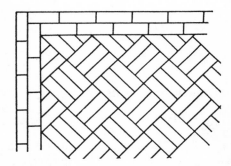

Figure 273　*Wood-blocks laid with basket-weave bond*

Some consist of a bituminous material which has
been suspended in a common liquid such as
water, and before the tiles can be laid, this liquid
must evaporate to leave the bituminous material
on the base concrete ready to receive the tiles.
When first laid the solution is brown but gradually
turns black. The floor-layer knows that tiles
should not be laid until the solution changes colour.

Plastic tiles are rarely identical to one another,
and manufacturers are usually only too willing to
give technical advice about their characteristics or
methods of laying, as a poorly laid floor is a bad
advertisement for their products.

All types of floor finishes should be protected
from damage by workmen's boots, heavy equipment with sharp edges, or staining caused by the
spilling of liquids. A good practice is to put a layer
of sawdust over the surface and place walking
boards over the top so that they are well clear of
the floor finish. It is unwise to lay a rough board
directly on top of a plastic-tile finish because any

irregularities in the board may be transferred to the surface of the tiles and will be extremely difficult to remove.

Painters working in the room should cover the surface of the floor with sheets to protect it against paint droppings or damage.

An oak floor should be well-covered if a bricklayer or a plasterer is working nearby on such operations as fixing sills or a fireplace surround, or plastering walls. Mortars, particularly those made with lime, and plasters cause bad staining which is either permanent or extremely difficult and costly to remove.

Self-assessment questions

1 When adopting the separate method of laying screeds the laitance should be
   (a) left on the surface to provide a key
   (b) removed before laying the screed
   (c) scratched to provide a key

2 Lightweight aggregates are used for screeds for
   (a) keeping the weight of the floor to a minimum
   (b) sound insulation
   (c) heat insulation

3 When using the monolithic method of laying a granolithic floor, the topping should be laid
   (a) 3 hours after laying the concrete slab
   (b) 5 hours after laying the concrete slab
   (c) 7 hours after laying the concrete slab

4 Wood-blocks are laid in
   (a) a cement and sand mortar screed 1:2 mix
   (b) an emulsified adhesive
   (c) hot pitch mastic

5 If a fall of 60 mm in 4 m is required and the straightedge is 2.75 m long, the fall in the length of the straightedge will be
   (a) 35.5 mm
   (b) 41.25 mm
   (c) 45.75 mm

6 Why are screeds generally laid on floors and roof slabs?

7 Why should the mix for a floor slab be not too wet for laying?

8 How can a non-slip surface be obtained on a granolithic floor?

9 Describe the laying of quarry tiles and their recommended treatment after laying.

10 Why is it so important to protect floor finishes after they have been laid? State the various methods of protection that may be used.

Chapter 16

Scaffolding

After reading this chapter you should be able to:

1   Understand the meaning of working 'overhand' and its advantages and disadvantages.

2   Have an understanding of the principles involved in erecting scaffolding, both dependent and independent.

3   Know the various terms applied to tubular scaffolding.

4   Know the reasons why scaffolding units should be carefully stored when not in use on the site.

5   Have an appreciation of the requirements of the safety regulations concerned with scaffolding.

6   Realize the importance of careful fixing of ladders and their storage when not in use.

Since brickwork is a constructive craft, it is continually developing and changing. As buildings develop in an upward direction, working platforms must be provided which are extended stage by stage to enable the craftsmen to reach their work, and to provide the means of conveying their materials. These platforms are called scaffolds.

There are two ways of building external walls. The first involves the erecting of a scaffold on the inside of the building only. So the cost of scaffolding for single-storey buildings is kept to a minimum because only one platform is needed. When the building has two or more storeys, scaffolds may be erected on each floor. In these cases less elaborate systems are needed than would be necessary for high scaffolds. When scaffolding is on one side of the wall only, the bricklayers work *overhand* in building the wall and pointing the joints as the work proceeds.

The second practice involves scaffolding all around the building as well as inside. This is rather more costly in actual scaffolding, but it allows the work to be done more quickly because men can work each side of the wall at the same time, commonly described as one *laying the face work* and the other *backing up*. The face work can also be pointed and cleaned down after the work is completed.

The scaffold material used on the outside of a building must be strong, durable, soundly erected, well-braced against possible collapse and securely tied into the building to prevent its falling outwards. Nowadays practically all scaffolding is constructed of metal – either steel or aluminium alloy. In special cases timber scaffolds are used.

Patent scaffold frames

Metal scaffolds may be constructed from patent welded units which are interlinked and secured together so as to form a large framework to support the scaffold platform. This type of frame allows for the speedy erection of a scaffold, but is not quite so flexible in design as the conventional tubular scaffold.

Tubular scaffolds

Metal scaffolds may be constructed of steel or aluminium alloy tubes connected together by means of special fittings or couplings. Aluminium alloy is becoming increasingly popular because of its lightness, which allows for ease of handling and transportation, but special care must be taken to ensure that such alloy tubes are not overloaded. Steel scaffolding is much stronger and therefore, will carry heavier loads, but in no case must scaffold platforms be loaded in such a way as to make them unsafe.

There are two ways in which tubular scaffolding may be erected:

1 *Dependent*, where the scaffold relies on the wall for support (Figure 274).

2 *Independent*, where the scaffold is erected so that it is self-supporting and is clear of the wall (Figure 275).

Scaffolding terms

The *standard* is the tube used as a vertical support in a scaffold. This transmits the load to the ground and should be fixed upright or slightly leaning towards the building (Figures 274 and 276).

The *ledger* is the horizontal tube which ties a scaffold longitudinally and acts as a support for putlogs or transoms. It should be fixed at right angles to the standard (Figures 274 and 275).

The *putlog* is the tube spanning the distance from the ledger to the wall of a building, upon which the boards rest (Figures 274 and 277).

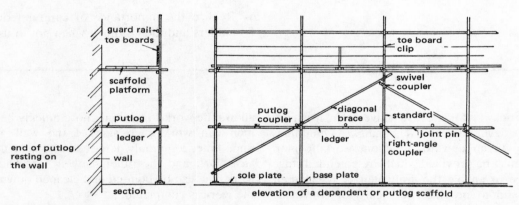

Figure 274   *Dependent scaffold*

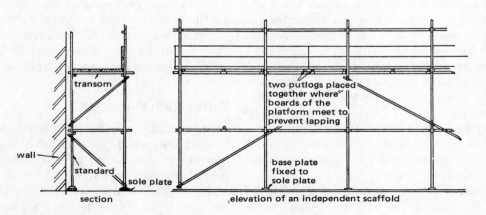

Figure 275   *Independent scaffold*

The *transom* is the tube spanning across two ledgers in an independent scaffold (Figure 275).

The *raker* is the tube which bears on the ground or an adjacent structure.

The *brace* is the tube fixed diagonally in a scaffold to prevent any movement (Figures 274 and 275).

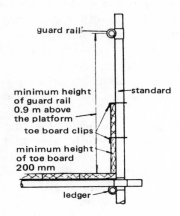

Figure 276 *Fixing guard rails and toeboards*

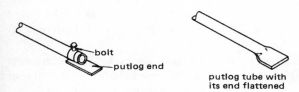

Figure 277 *Two types of putlogs*

The *reveal tie* is the tube which is wedged between two solid surfaces such as door jambs or window reveals to tie a scaffold to a building (Figure 278).

The *tie* is the tube which connects a scaffold to a reveal tie or other rigid anchorage (Figure 278).

The *bridle* is the horizontal tube supported from putlogs at a window opening, supporting intermediate putlogs.

The *right-angle coupler* connects a standard and a ledger (Figure 274).

The *putlog coupler* is the non-load-bearing fit-

ting and is used for fixing a putlog or transom to a ledger (Figure 279).

The *swivel coupler* connects two tubes at any angle that may be required. It would be used to connect a brace to a standard or ledger (Figure 280).

The *sleeve coupler* is the connector which fits on the outside of the tube and joins two tubes together end-to-end.

The *joint pin* or *spigot* also connects two tubes together but is an internal fitting, and is more commonly used than the sleeve coupler.

The *reveal pin* is used for tightening a reveal tie between two jambs (Figure 278).

The *base plate* is used at the base of a standard and should have a bearing surface of at least 0.0225 m^2 (Figure 281).

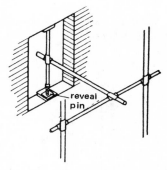

Figure 278 *Method of tying-in a scaffold with the aid of a reveal pin*

Plastic plugs are mushroom-headed plastic units which are inserted into the ends of exposed scaffold tubes to give protection against people hitting their heads on the ends of the tubes.

Safety regulations

It is essential that scaffolds be erected under the supervision of a competent person so that they conform to the requirements of the Construction (Working Places) Regulations No. 94 and the Construction (General Provisions) regulations 1580 and 1581, which are the relevant sections of the Health and Safety at Work etc. Act.

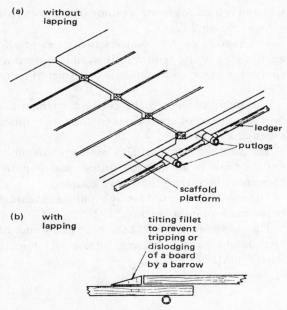

Figure 279   *Methods of placing boards on a scaffold platform with lapping and without lapping*

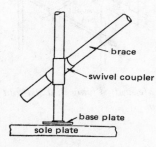

Figure 280   *Application of a swivel coupling*

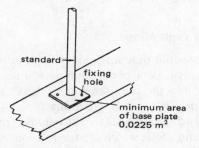

Figure 281   *Base plate*

The accident rate in the building industry is very high indeed and you should take every precaution to reduce it. Most accidents are caused through falls or falling objects. It is most necessary to erect scaffolds in such a manner as to prevent either of these types of accident from occurring.

Scaffolds should be inspected regularly to ensure that they are in a sound condition, rigid, and fit for the purpose of carrying men and materials. The results of such inspections should be entered in a register and defects, if any, should be noted, as well as the action that has been taken to correct the defects.

The standards should rest on a solid base, preferably on base plates. Never use loose bricks or packing.

The distances between putlogs depend upon the thickness of the boards being used.

Thickness of board	The distance apart should not exceed
30 mm	1 m
37 mm	1.5 m
50 mm	2.5 m

Platforms should be closely boarded, and the end of a board should not overlap a putlog by more than four times its thickness. The width of platforms should be at least 0.625 m if for footing only, and 0.85 m if materials are to be deposited on it.

Toeboards must be provided on all platforms higher than 2 m. They must be at least 200 mm above the top of the platform (Figure 276).

Guard rails must be set at least 0.900 m above the platform and fixed on the inside of the standards. The space between the toeboard and guard rail should not exceed 0.68 m (Figure 276).

Ladders must be of sound construction and have no defective or missing rungs. When using a ladder, secure it firmly at the top, rest it on a solid base and pass it at least 0.900 m beyond the platform.

Leave openings in toeboard and handrails where the ladders are fixed to provide a means of access.

Safety of personnel
1   Never use makeshift scaffolding.

2 Never take risks on scaffolds.
3 Never use sub-quality or defective equipment.
4 Never leave spanners lying around for people to interfere with scaffolding.
5 Scaffolding should never be altered, or putlogs, transoms and toeboards removed except by the people responsible for the scaffolding.
6 Keep scaffold platforms clear and tidy, as loose materials or tools lying on the platform can easily cause a person to trip or stumble, which might make him fall right off the scaffold.
7 Always use a ladder when coming down from a scaffold; never clamber down the scaffolding.

Trestle scaffolds

These are a useful type of scaffold where speedy erection is required but they must not have more than three tiers and the working platform must never be more than 4.5 metres above the ground or floor on which the trestle scaffold rests. Fix and brace trestles securely.

Care of equipment

Keep scaffold fittings tidily in bins or underneath racks, and never leave them lying around the job in mud or rubbish. Take care of these fittings – they are expensive items. After completion of the job, it is a good practice to dip them in an oil or mixture of oil and paraffin and allow to drain before stacking away.

Stack poles in racks (Figures 282) or in pegged spaces on boards (Figure 283). Never stack them adjacent to a road as lorries may run over them; or loosely on top of one another as a nasty accident can occur if somebody treads on the stack and the poles roll away, causing a fall. When a job is finished and the steel scaffolding is going back in store, it is a good plan to clean off any rust and paint with a red oxide paint, or dip in an oil bath and allow to drain before stacking.

Ladders

Never hang ladders so that they rest on the upper stiles, but on the lower stiles (Figure 284). Never paint ladders in such a way that any defects are hidden. It is usually better to varnish ladders.

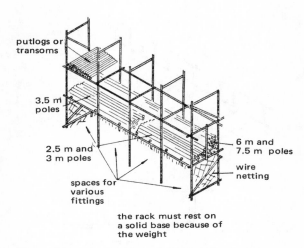

Figure 282 *A suitable rack for storing scaffold tubes and fittings*

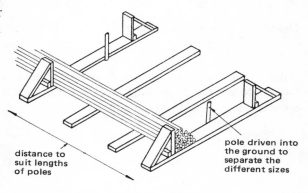

Figure 283 *Stacking tubes on boards*

Never nail a piece of wood on the front of a ladder to replace a broken rung. Never allow ladders to fall heavily, but always lower them gently to the ground.

Boards

Stack boards flat and tidily to prevent them from becoming twisted or distorted, which will happen if they are stacked in an untidy fashion and subjected to uneven forces. Never throw boards down from scaffolding; the force of hitting the ground is likely to split them. Should scaffold boards become badly twisted or split through mishandling do not use them on scaffolds as they

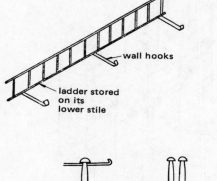

wall hooks

ladder stored
on its
lower stile

incorrect
method of
storing
ladders as
the weight
tends to
loosen the
rungs

correct method,
as this creates no
strain on the
rungs or stiles

Figure 284   *Storing a ladder*

will be a danger to any person working on them. Good storage and stacking are essential for economic use of scaffold equipment.

Self-assessment questions

1   A 'ledger' is the tube which is
   (a)   the vertical support of a scaffold
   (b)   the cross-brace of a scaffold
   (c)   the horizontal member of a scaffold

2   A 'transom' is the
   (a)   horizontal member which has one end resting on the wall and upon which the boards rest
   (b)   horizontal tube 'tying in' a scaffold at an opening
   (c)   horizontal tube resting on two supports and upon which the boards rest

3   A 'sleeve coupler' is a
   (a)   connector which joins two tubes end-to-end externally
   (b)   connector which joins two tubes end-to-end internally
   (c)   connector which secures a putlog to the ledger

4   If 37 mm thick scaffold boards are used for a platform, then the maximum distance between the supports must be
   (a)   1.0 m
   (b)   1.5 m
   (c)   2.0 m

5   The minimum width of platforms if materials are to be deposited on them is
   (a)   0.625 m
   (b)   0.750 m
   (c)   0.850 m

6   Toeboards must be provided on all platforms which are higher than
   (a)   1.5 m
   (b)   2.0 m
   (c)   2.5 m

7   The space between the guard rail and the toeboard must not exceed
   (a)   0.68 m
   (b)   0.73 m
   (c)   0.78 m

8   Trestle scaffolds may be taken to a height of
   (a)   3.5 m
   (b)   4.5 m
   (c)   5.0 m

9   Ladders must be securely tied at the top and project above the platform at least
   (a)   0.7 m
   (b)   0.8 m
   (c)   0.9 m

10   Describe how a scaffold may be 'tied' into a building.

Chapter 17

Boundary walls

After reading this chapter you should be able to:

1 Understand why adequate foundations must be provided at the base of boundary walls.

2 Know how to increase the stability of boundary walling.

3 Know how to erect gate pillars and bond them into boundary walling, and know how to fix various types of cappings.

4 Know how to fix ornamental ironwork.

5 Know how to construct straight and circular ramps.

There must always be adequate foundations provided at the base of boundary walls to resist frost, wind and rain. Although this type of walling is not usually required to withstand heavy loads acting in a downward direction, it is subject to other forces, such as:

The movement of soil under the foundations.

The pressure of earth if it should be piled up behind the wall – this may happen where gardens on sloping sites are levelled up and the earth is piled up behind the boundary wall.

Wind pressure on the face of the wall.

Foundations

These should be thick enough to prevent cracking when the weight of the wall or any other pressures are acting upon them. They should also be deep enough to remain unaffected by drying shrinkage, which may occur in the soil above and under the foundation. Some types of soil, particularly clays, expand when they become wet, and shrink when they dry out. This movement is more pronounced near the surface where the soil is more likely to be subjected to temperature changes, and decreases according to the level at which the particular soil retains a reasonably consistent moisture content.

For this same reason trees should never be planted immediately adjacent to walls, and par-

ticularly never in clay soils because they increase the drying shrinkage by extracting the moisture rapidly out of the gound. The continual movement of subsoil underneath foundations is liable to cause cracking in them and, as a result of this, in the walling above. It is therefore necessary to take the level of the foundations deep enough to resist this continual movement in the ground.

Attached piers

For economic reasons, boundary walls are usually built with thin walling, and it therefore becomes necessary to strengthen them by thickening at intervals with buttresses or attached piers. These piers help to prevent the wall from overturning when a great pressure is being exerted on one face of the wall, but for these piers to be completely effective they should be taken up to within a distance from the top of the wall equal to three times the least thickness of the wall. Attached piers should not be less than 100 mm thick and must be bonded into the wall to which they are attached in order to achieve the maximum support from the pier. Figures 285–291 show bonding arrangements for attached piers in stretcher, English and Flemish bonds.

Tumbling-in. The tops of the attached piers may be finished off by turning the pier into the wall so that a weathering is formed and a decorative feature effected. This is called *tumbling-in*. Figures 292 and 293 show examples of the methods to use in this work.

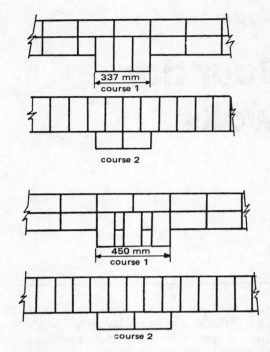

Figure 286 *Bonding attached piers in English bond*

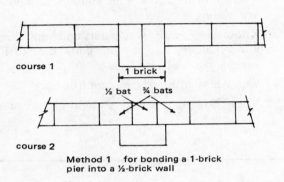

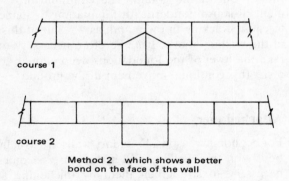

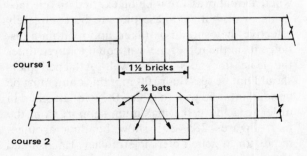

Figure 285 *Bonding attached piers into a wall built in stretcher bond*

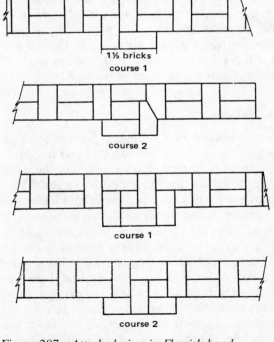

Figure 287 *Attached piers in Flemish bond*

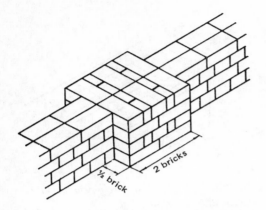

Figure 288   *Double attached piers in English bond*

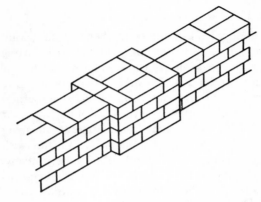

Figure 291   *Double attached piers in Flemish bond*

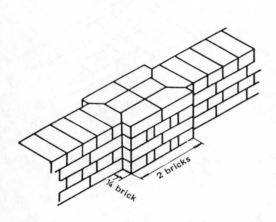

Figure 289   *Double attached piers in English bond*

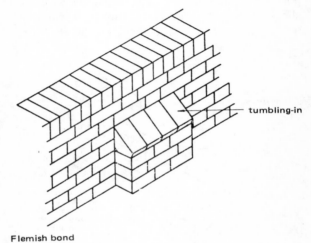

Flemish bond

Figure 292   *Tumbling-in*

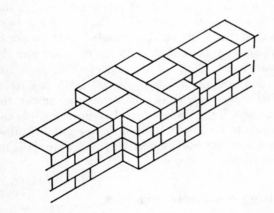

Figure 290   *Double attached piers in Flemish bond*

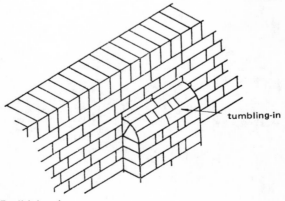

English bond

Figure 293   *Tumbling-in*

Gate pillars

A boundary wall should be thickened at any point where a gate is to be hung, so that it is strong enough to resist the forces which are exerted by the gate on the wall. This thickening for the gate pier is another form of attached pier. One method of constructing these piers is to build an outer shell in brickwork, then place some reinforcing rods in the space in the middle and fill this with concrete (Figures 294 and 295). Alternatively, the pier may be built in solid brickwork. (Figures 296 and 297 show methods of bonding these types of piers in English and Flemish bonds.)

Fixing for gates. When the pier is being built the position of the hinge brackets should be carefully checked from the gates which are to be hung on them. They may be built in the pier as the work

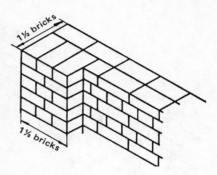

Figure 296   *A 1½-brick square pier attached to a 1-brick wall in Flemish bond*

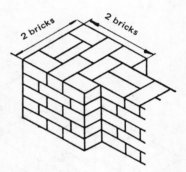

Figure 297   *A 2-brick square pier attached to a 1-brick wall in Flemish bond*

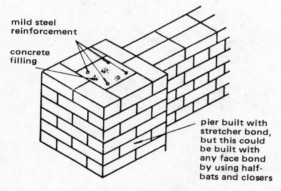

Figure 294   *An attached pier suitable for supporting a heavy gate*

proceeds, but great care must be taken to ensure that they are absolutely plumb on all exposed faces, otherwise the gate will not swing correctly, or it will be out of level. Alternatively, the brackets may be fixed after the pier is built and in this case sand courses are left in the pier at the position of the brackets. To fix the brackets the bricks which were bedded in sand are removed and the sand brushed out of the holes; these are dampened and the brackets placed in their correct positions. The brickwork around and above the brackets is then bedded in place ensuring that the brackets are solidly built in the pier, and fixed so that they are truly plumb with each other (Figure 298).

Fixing ornamental ironwork

Sometimes wrought-ironwork is required to be

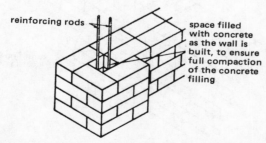

Figure 295   *An alternative method of reinforcing a gate pier*

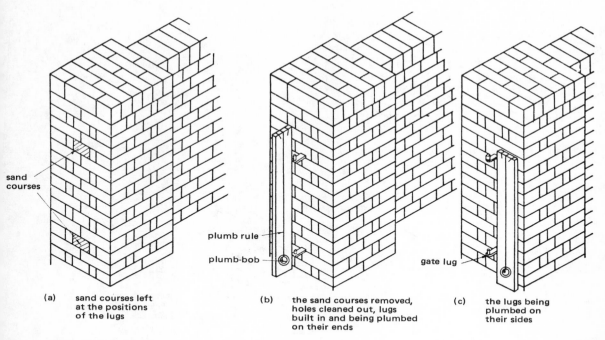

(a) sand courses left at the positions of the lugs

plumb rule

plumb-bob

(b) the sand courses removed, holes cleaned out, lugs built in and being plumbed on their ends

gate lug

(c) the lugs being plumbed on their sides

Figure 298 *Fixing gate hinges*

fixed on the top of low boundary walls; this type of wrought-ironwork may be fixed by building lugs into the walling or by drilling holes in the wall and filling solidly with white bronze plugs or lead wool plugs, to which the metal-work is fixed with brass screws.

Pier capping

Gate piers should be finished off with a capping to protect the pier against the weather and to form a decorative feature. Figure 299 shows a brick-on-edge and tile creasing for a 2-brick square pier. Figure 300 shows a mitred brick capping which involves a considerable amount of cutting, but once the angles of the cuts have been determined it presents little or no difficulty if a mechanical brick or masonry saw is available.

Figure 301 shows typical stone cappings suitable for a gate pier.

Wall capping

Figure 302 illustrates various types of capping that may be used for boundary walls.

Figure 299 *Brick-on-edge and tile-creasing capping*

Figure 300 *Mitred brick-on-edge capping*

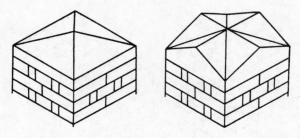

Figure 301   *Types of stone capping suitable for piers*

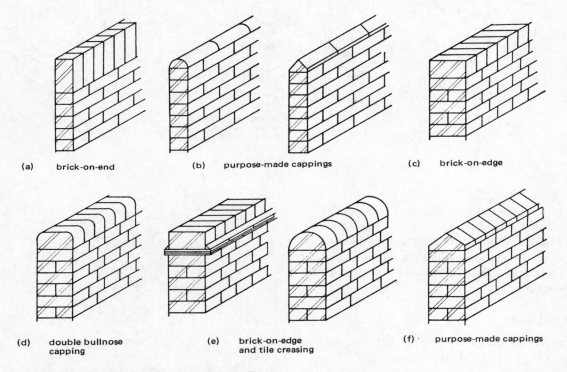

| (a) | brick-on-end | (b) | purpose-made cappings | (c) | brick-on-edge |

| (d) | double bullnose capping | (e) | brick-on-edge and tile creasing | (f) | purpose-made cappings |

Figure 302   *Suitable cappings for boundary walls*

Ramps

Another decorative feature may be introduced into a boundary wall where it joins a gate pillar and is finished at a lower level than the pillar, by building a ramp. To set out a straight ramp fix a line (Figure 303), mark the bricks with a bevel (see Chapter 3), cut them with a hammer and bolster or mechanical saw and bed them to the line. Raise the line to bed each course of tiles and

the brick-on-edge. The brick-on-edge should be mitred at the angles. The mitre should bisect the angle of the ramp (Figure 304).

This is the method of building a circular ramp. Erect the pier to the height of the top of the ramp. Place a length of timber of suitable size (75 × 50 mm would be adequate) and long enough to extend beyond the striking point of the curve. Place dry bricks on top of this timber to weight it down and keep it in place (Figure 306). Fix a thin

length of wood, 25 by 6 mm, equal in length to
the radius plus about 400 mm, at the striking
point of the curve of the ramp. This is called a
trammel. The work is simplified if the trammel is
sawn to a point at the free end, because the pencil
marking of the bricks to be cut is kept on the
centre line of the trammel, which makes the setting out as accurate as possible.

After the ramp has been prepared for the
bricks-on-edge refix the trammel at a distance
equal to the brick-on-edge plus one joint, and lay
the brick-on-edge coping to the trammel (Figures
307 and 308).

If the radius of the ramp is small, cut the bricks
wedge-shaped in the same manner for cutting
arch voussoirs, but if the radius is large then possibly you should build the ramp with vee joints,
although this will mainly depend upon the quality
of the work required.

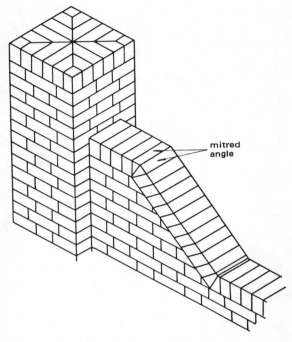

Figure 304   *Method of cutting and preparing a ramp to
a boundary wall*

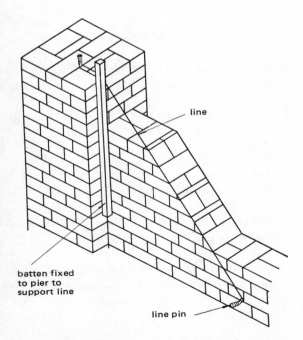

Figure 303   *Method of cutting and preparing a ramp
for a brick-on-edge ramp*

Figure 305   *Brick-on-edge and tile-creasing capping to
a ramp*

Stage 1

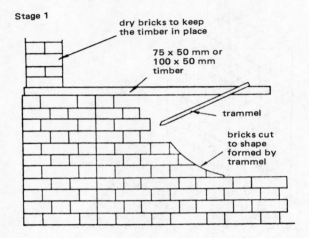

Figure 306   *Building a circular ramp*
The ramp is built up and the trammel fixed at its correct distance for the cutting of the brickwork to receive the brick-on-edge

Stage 2

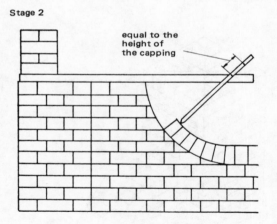

Figure 307   *Completing the circular ramp*
When the brickwork cutting is complete, the trammel is refixed at a distance equal to the capping, and the capping is laid to the curve of the ramp with the aid of the trammel

Stage 3

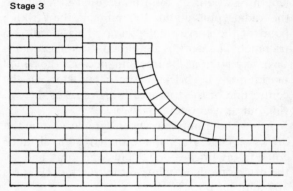

Figure 308   *The brick-on-edge capping is complete*

Self-assessment questions

1   What forces does a boundary wall have to withstand?

2   Describe the methods that are used to strengthen the wall against these forces.

3   Explain why trees should not be planted adjacent to walling, particularly in clay soils.

4   With the aid of neat sketches show how attached piers may be finished off at the top.

5   Describe the methods that may be used for fixing gate hinge brackets.

6   Show two methods of capping
    (a)   a gate pier
    (b)   a boundary wall

7   Describe a method of cutting a straight ramp for a boundary wall.

8   State the operations which are involved in cutting a circular ramp for a boundary wall.

Index

Note
The following bibliography has been referred to in the text and readers are recommended to pursue their studies by further reading of this literature.

Building Research Station Digests
BS 12   Portland cement
BS 130 Engineering bricks
BS 187 Sand-lime bricks
BS 882 Aggregates
BS 890 Limes
BS 1180 Concrete bricks
The Building Regulations
Health and Safety at Work etc. Act
The Protection of Eyes
   Regulations
The Construction (Working
   Places) Regulations No. 94